STOLEN GLORY

THE U.S., THE SOVIET UNION, AND THE OLYMPIC BASKETBALL GAME THAT NEVER ENDED

Chris —
Go I.U.
Hope you enjoy —
Taps

MIKE BREWSTER AND TA

Published in the United States by GM Books,
Los Angeles, California.

Library of Congress Cataloging-in-Publication Data

Mike Brewster & Taps Gallagher

Stolen Glory

GMBooks.com
Los Angeles – Hong Kong
325 N. Maple Dr.
Beverly Hills, CA 90210
(310) 475-2988

ISBN #1882383796
1 2 4 6 8 9 7 5 3

Book Design: Mark Heliger
Cover Design: Chloe Bartholomew
Editor: Paul Rogers
Project Director: William Dorich

Printed in USA

Dedication

For my wife, Kim, whose understanding, patience and support allowed me to take this wonderful journey back in time.

For my daughters, Glynis, Morgan and Nell who have listened to the same stories over and over again with a smile on their faces–I love and thank you all.

–TG

For Lucy, Francie and Charlie, who can make anything–even writing a book–fun.

–MB

CONTENTS

PROLOGUE:
Three Seconds from Gold

This book is, ostensibly, about a single basketball game. Officially, the Soviet Union beat the United States, 51-50, in the gold medal game at the 1972 Summer Olympic Games in Munich on a desperate basket at the final buzzer.

In many ways, the game was for the Soviets a mirror image of what the U.S. Olympic hockey team would experience eight years later at the Winter Games in Lake Placid: an improbable, almost unthinkable, victory over the sport's long-time Olympic standard-bearers and a Cold War shot in the arm for a politically struggling government.

But that is where the similarities end. Because there's one Olympian-sized difference between what is, arguably, each country's greatest Olympic achievement: the Soviets didn't actually *win* the gold medal in basketball in 1972. Or, more specifically, they have never been recognized as having won by their American opponents. To this day, 40 years after that final buzzer sounded, 12 silver medals lay unclaimed in a storage room maintained for the Olympic Museum in Lausanne, Switzerland. History says those silver medals belong to the Americans. Doug Collins and his teammates say that "history" is mistaken.

Why do Collins, the sparkplug of the '72 team and now the head coach of the Philadelphia 76ers, and his former teammates—all of whom are still alive—continue to insist the gold medals were wrongly awarded to the Soviet Union?

To understand, it helps to go back to Benton, Illinois just for a moment, where Collins would imagine countless times what it would be like to sink a historic winning basket. In his mind, he was playing in the state championship for the Benton High Rangers or in the NCAA title game for Illinois State (the alma mater of his high school coach and the school Collins would attend, too). Or, just maybe, he would hit those shots someday in the NBA finals. The whip-thin, 130-pound high school sophomore would always use the same routine as he practiced shooting that pair of free throws that would make history: Bounce the ball three times. Spin it in his hands. Shoot.

But Collins never could have imagined what would transpire in the wee hours of September 10, 1972, in Munich, West Germany, just days after the kidnapping and murder of 11 Israeli athletes and coaches by Palestinian terrorists, an atrocity that led Olympic officials to consider cancelling the rest of the Games. With three seconds remaining on the clock, Collins stood at the free throw line for the United States of America, with his team, after mounting a heroic comeback, down by one point to the Soviet Union in the Olympic gold medal game. Collins, as it happened, couldn't even see straight. Moments earlier, after making a spectacular open-court steal from one of the best Soviet players, he had been knocked out cold as he drove the lane for a potential game-winning layup.

In his haze, a bruise welling under his left eye, Collins grabbed the aching left wrist on which he had landed and tried to gather his faculties. Confusion reigned as assistant coaches scrambled to find a player they trusted to replace Collins and shoot the two free throws. That's when Collins heard the team's 68-year-old head coach, Hank Iba, say in his trademark raspy tone: "If Doug can walk, he's going to shoot." It was the last game Iba ever coached in a long and celebrated career—and one of the best moves he ever made.

Collins blocked everything out: the crowd, his injuries, the Cold War, the potential gold medal. He was trying to become that kid on the playground again. He had come full-circle: the schoolboy who imagined being in the big game became the Olympian who imagined being back in the schoolyard. "I thought about the one thing that I had always counted on regardless of the situation," Collins says. "Three dribbles, spin, and shoot it."**

Even though their loyalties had seemed divided throughout the game, the 6,500 spectators crammed into Munich's *basketballhalle* cheered wildly as Collins made both free throws to put the U.S. ahead, 50-49. Olympic gold seemingly belonged to the Americans. But after the Soviets' first unsuccessful attempt at scoring during the last three ticks of the clock, they were given another chance to inbound, because of reasons still disputed to this day. When the Soviets failed on their second attempt, the ball harmlessly bouncing off the backboard, the U.S. players erupted at midcourt, jumping up and down with their arms raised in triumph. This was the era, long before the strict stadium security of today, when fans would storm the court or playing field after a championship game, and sure enough they swarmed the American team. One fan tried to pull off Tom Henderson's jersey; another stole Iba's wallet. ABC's Frank Gifford, calling the game for TV viewers back in the States, announced that the U.S. had capped an unlikely comeback. The game was over. Collins, the man, had fulfilled his boyhood dream, and on the biggest stage of all. He had sunk two foul shots that instantly made history.

Except, fantastically, they would not. As the American team rejoiced, the head of FIBA, basketball's international ruling body, ordered that the Soviets be given a *third* chance to take the ball out of bounds.

This time, Aleksandr Belov, the Soviet player who earlier had let his poor pass be filched by Collins, leapt high in the air to catch a full-court heave from a teammate, shed two U.S. defenders, one on either side of him, and laid the ball into the basket.

Belov, arms aloft, sprinted all the way to the other side of the court to be enveloped by his teammates, all dressed in Soviet-issue red jerseys. The Soviet players rolled around on the floor, hugging each other as well as their coaches and trainers, and swigging from bottles of vodka that had appeared out of nowhere.

The scene in the Americans' locker room moments later was chaotic. Some players were despondent; others gathered to form a plan. Soon, they all agreed: if the protest they would file did not result in the Soviets' victory being overturned, the American players would refuse to accept the silver medals. Forty years later, say Collins and many of his teammates, what hurts the most is the memory of that celebration at midcourt, the euphoric moment when they felt and believed they had won.

So while this book is indeed about that 40-minute basketball game and all its Cold War build-up 40 years ago, it is also about an agonizing choice that was made in the immediate confusing aftermath by a dozen young men, none over the age of 23, and how that decision has reverberated through the years. After all, 40 years is a long time. The Berlin Wall was toppled, the Iron Curtain pulled back. The Soviet Union no longer exists and the Cold War has been relegated to history books, Americans' biggest international fears now trained on the War on Terror.

But despite the march of time, one thing hasn't changed. As a team—and that is the only way the International Olympic Committee will allow the silver medals to be awarded—the Americans today insist they want nothing to do with the silver medals. The pain of that dreamlike, five-minute celebration still haunts them. In fact, the players, led by Tom McMillen, who after his basketball career went on to serve in Congress, have lent their support to a grass-roots movement to try to convince the IOC to retroactively award the American team duplicate gold medals. A precedent for such a move was set for the Canadian pairs figure skaters at the 2002 Winter Games in Salt Lake City after a scandal committed by an Olympic judge was determined to have deprived them of their rightful gold.

For the Soviets, their basketball victory in 1972 quickly took on a mystical and spiritual air. A woman who was the Soviets' "house mother," helping to cook and clean for the team, began to share her Christian beliefs with the Soviet players. Mostly they nodded and were polite; the Soviet government was infamous for persecuting Christians as well as Jews.

On the night before the gold medal game, however, the Soviets' house mother preached the Gospel to the players, beseeching them to believe. One player thanked her and said, "I will believe in your God if you will pray for us to win the gold medal." The house mother replied that she couldn't do that but would pray that God reveal himself in some way. After the Soviets won the gold medal game, this same player returned to the house and said that now that the Games were over and his team had triumphed, he believed in God and accepted Jesus as his savior. His name? Aleksandr Belov. Belov died just six years later.

In death, Belov is still an Olympic gold medal winner. In life, 40 years later, the Americans still believe they won the game, and they still want their own gold medals. Four decades later, they are still three seconds from gold.

**Unless otherwise indicated, all interviews cited in this book were conducted by the authors.

Acknowledgments and Sources

This book could not have been written without the 12 members of the 1972 Olympic men's basketball team. All of the players carved time out from their schedules to sit for interviews and answer follow-up questions to make sure that we got the story right. Interviews with assistant coach Johnny Bach, and subsequent conversations with him, were critical as well.

A number of other people with varying degrees of connection to the team also agreed to be interviewed, and we are sincerely grateful for that involvement. They include, in no particular order: Bobby Knight, Dennis Lewin, Frank Gifford, the late Gene Bartow, Moe Iba, Mary Haskins, Brent Haskins, Mike D'Antoni, and Mary Siedman. Several prominent members of the basketball community assisted us in various ways, among them Barry Parkhill, Bill Wall, John Brown, Swen Nater, Peter Halpin, Lefty Driesell, Brian Winters and Ed Klimkowski. Thanks also to Donna Mathis, Taps' assistant, without whose dedication and support this book would have never gone to press.

Also many thanks to Steve Rogers, Bob Deist, Steve Morse, Butch Gallagher and John Ostojic for listening to Taps' tale for the past four years and supporting this project.

Finally, a million thank you's to researcher Jack O'Hara, who single-handedly located all of the players and participants for this book and helped make the dream come true.

x

Our editor, Paul Rogers—also a good friend—became an important member of the team within days. With his editorial skills, ear for language and affability, Paul is the ideal person to come in cold and greatly improve a text. Thanks again to Paul for a great job.

For other favors great and small, a big thank you to Sam Freedman, Allan Heye, Doug Heye, Amada Schwer, Mark Svenvold, Martha McPhee, Janet Odgis and Chloe Bartholomew. Mike would also like to thank Amey Stone for her constant support, as well as Lucy, Francie, and Charlie for their enthusiasm and patience.

In terms of sources, several excellent books informed our work, including *American Hoops: U.S. Men's Olympic Basketball from Berlin to Beijing,* by Carson Cunningham; *Giant Steps,* by Kareem Abdul-Jabbar; *From Set Shot to Slam Dunk: the Glory Days of Basketball in the Words of Those who Played it,* by Charles Salzberg; and *Munich 1972: Sport, Politics and Tragedy,* a dissertation by Christopher Clark Elzey. All of these works have been credited and duly noted in the text when we cite their ideas and analysis.

Part 1:

The Russians Are Coming

CHAPTER 1

The Game the World Wanted to See

The basketball game with the strangest ending in Olympic history began under highly unusual circumstances as well.

The attack by Palestinian terrorists that four days earlier claimed the lives of 11 Israeli athletes and coaches made an afterthought of the remainder of the Olympic program. Barring an extraordinary series of events, the gold medal game between the Americans and the Soviets would quickly fade into memory. Several of the U.S. players at the time felt that, out of respect to the victims of the massacre, the game should not even be played.

Moreover, the deciding contest was scheduled for the absurd hour of 11:45 P.M. on a Saturday night, which created the dual effect of having 24 sluggish players and 6,500 frenzied fans in the arena a few miles south of Munich. Two years earlier, FIBA, the international basketball governing body, and the Munich Olympic organizing committee had agreed to a request for the late starting time from ABC. From the players' standpoint, beginning the game at a quarter to midnight was simply "too late," recalled Ed Ratleff, the U.S.A.'s All-America forward from Long Beach State: "You're trying not to do a lot of things, you can't eat too much, and you're just thinking about it all day."

Even though ABC had requested the late starting time so the network could broadcast the game in prime time back in the States, ABC ultimately didn't show the game live. Tip-off was at 5:45 P.M. Eastern daylight time, Saturday, September 9. With the contest complete by the time ABC's evening coverage of the Olympics began, the network could edit the game footage and mix in the day's other highlights that Roone Arledge—the man who would go on to make the Olympics must-watch TV—wanted in his prime-time programming. It would take some facile editing under pressure by ABC producers, but it could be done. ABC had perfected this medley style of sports coverage in its hugely popular Saturday afternoon show, *Wide*

World of Sports, featuring everything from cliff diving to water skiing to boxing.

Players exchanging gifts prior to the start of the gold medal game, September 9, 1972.
(Courtesy of Herbert J. Mols family).

By 21st-century standards, the idea that American viewers couldn't watch the Olympic gold medal basketball game live seems ridiculous. As then-ABC sportscaster Frank Gifford, who called the game with Bill Russell, marveled in retrospect: "It's hard to believe how primitive everything was back then." But even several years after the Munich Games, many major sporting events were shown on tape delay. Throughout the 1970s, the NBA playoffs and finals were often tape-delayed, as was the "Miracle on Ice," the improbable U.S. victory over the Soviets in ice hockey in the 1980 Olympic Games in Lake Placid. Locals on the streets of the tiny Adirondack village in upstate New York celebrated for more than an hour before the national television audience witnessed the conclusion of the historic game.

When the time finally came for the tip-off in Munich, there was one last surprise. The Soviets' second-leading scorer, Modestas Paulauskas, wasn't in the starting lineup. Even though Paulauskas was a strong post player, the Soviet coaches opted for speed and quickness to cope with U.S. guards Tom Henderson, Doug Collins and Kevin Joyce. The other four Soviet starters, though, were the familiar stalwarts of the Red Army team.

In terms of age and experience, the Soviet team bore more comparison to one of the NBA or ABA clubs the Americans had played in exhibitions than to any other Olympic team the U.S. had faced in Munich. The Soviets were led by Sergei Belov, one of the best guards in Europe, who had been playing for a top Russian club team since 1964 when he was 20 years old. Belov, a hard-nosed, intelligent and sweet-shooting player, would go on to coach the Russian national team after the breakup of the Soviet Union.

The other star to watch on the Soviet squad was Aleksandr Belov, a big, athletic forward who could have played for any team in the NBA. The U.S. team even had a nickname for Aleksandr Belov: "Billy Cunningham," after the Philadelphia 76ers forward who was an excellent all-around player and, like Belov, not afflicted with "white man's disease"—in other words, he could jump. (Incidentally, despite the fact that only about half of the players on the U.S.S.R. team actually hailed from Russia, Gifford referred to the Soviet team as the "Russians" throughout. Paulauskas, for example, was a Lithuanian star who had won Lithuania's "Sportsman of the Year" award seven of the last eight years. Another key player in the final game was Zurab Sakandelidze, from the Republic of Georgia).

The Soviets were coached by Vladimir Kondrashin, who had replaced his archrival in the Soviet domestic league, Aleksandr Gomelsky, because a Gomelsky-coached national team had finished third in the 1970 World Basketball Championships. (In his 2005 book *Crashing the Borders*, Harvey Araton of the *New York Times* contended that the actual reason for Gomelsky's demotion was that the KGB suspected the Jewish Gomelsky was planning to defect to the Israeli delegation during the Games.)

The nature of the Soviet mandate to defeat America in basketball was summed up by Tom McMillen, the 6-foot-11 Renaissance man of the 1972 U.S. team who would go on to become a Rhodes Scholar and a congressman from Maryland. "This was really the Cold War being played out in Munich, Germany, at midnight, September 9, 1972," McMillen said. "It was so important for the Soviets to show some kind of superiority because at the time they were fighting against the U.S., which was superior economically, probably superior militarily. They had to keep some kind of hope alive for their people."

The starting lineup for the U.S. included Henderson, the team's floor general who just months before had been a relatively unknown junior college player; defensive stalwart Bobby Jones of the University of North Carolina; Dwight Jones, the dynamic Houston star who was leading in scoring at 9.6

points per game; Jim Brewer, the center who had averaged seven blocks a game for the University of Minnesota; and the All-America Ratleff, who could create his own shot as well as anyone on the team. Joyce and Collins, both of whom were excellent scorers, came off the bench. So did Jim Forbes, an alternate who had been picked when another player, John Brown, broke his foot during training camp in Pearl Harbor, and McMillen, the University of Maryland star who had played several strong games in the Olympics so far.

Henry "Hank" Iba, who had led the 1964 and 1968 U.S. Olympic teams to gold medals with his trademark deliberate offense, was coaching what everyone knew would be the last game of his career. Iba's storied 36-year run as head coach of Oklahoma State had come to an end two years earlier, after an unremarkable 14-12 season (which put his overall collegiate coaching record at 767-338). By the time the 1972 Games rolled around, Iba was a 68-year-old retiree who was two generations removed from his players chronologically and light years away from them in his basketball philosophy, which required four or five passes on every possession. "We were all interchangeable, and coach Iba made us feel that way," recalled Mike Bantom, a forward on the 1972 Olympic team. "We were to run the ball up the floor, pass it to the baseline, pass it back out and pass it about three or four other times before we shot. It didn't matter if you were open, you could run up and down the floor and be wide open. Unless you had a layup, you better not shoot that ball."

As the players gathered at center court for the jump ball—the Soviets in their plain red uniforms adorned only by numbers (not even a utilitarian "CCCP") and the Americans in white with "USA" emblazoned across their chests—the late-night crowd brimmed with excitement. Each team's starters didn't shake hands with or otherwise acknowledge their opponents. Brewer, who was extremely effective at keeping his blocks in play instead of swatting them out of bounds, stuffed an opponent on the very first possession after the Soviets had won the tip. Then Ratleff hit a cutting Bobby Jones with a beautiful bounce pass, a textbook Iba play that would have put the U.S. in front and completed a perfect start to the game on both ends of the court—only Jones missed the layup.

Brewer blocked his second shot on the Soviets' next possession, meaning he had two more blocks than either team had points. But Aleksandr

4

Belov followed up and was fouled. He made one of two free throws and the Soviets took the lead, 1-0. The next few possessions revealed the Americans were even more out of it than the Soviets at the late hour. Sakandelidze, whom Russell called the "fastest player in Europe," made a steal and blazed to the basket, getting fouled and hitting two free throws. A lazy pass by Henderson and another Sakandelidze steal and easy layup made it 5-0. After three minutes, the U.S. remained scoreless and looked horrendous on offense. While trying to adhere to Iba's rule of completing at least three passes before shooting, the U.S. players had become indecisive, turning the ball over in some of the ugliest ways possible. The Americans had routed so many teams during the Olympic tournament—including Egypt and Japan by more than 60 points apiece—that the deliberate style of play Iba preached hadn't been much of a factor. But now, playing tentatively against a physical and quick defensive team and unaccustomed to creating shots from offensive sets, the U.S. players were left to pass the ball around the perimeter until one of the Soviets cut in for a steal.

The Americans finally scored their first field goal when Ratleff made it 7-3 on a layup off a feed from Brewer. But no sooner did the Americans show some life than 28-year-old Sergei Belov took charge. The shooting guard had averaged just over 13 points in the previous eight games, but that statistic was misleading. With the Soviets registering so many blowouts, he hadn't needed to score much. He hit two free throws, stuck a jumper off the dribble, hit another from the top of the key, and then scored yet again from the outside for a 15-7 Soviet lead. The Americans were quickly seeing why Belov was, by 1972, already known as the Jerry West of Europe. Henderson was hands-down the Americans' toughest backcourt defender, and Belov was shooting as if Henderson weren't even there. "He was kicking my butt," Henderson recalled. "He was a grown man. You know that's his job. He was very basic, but he was smart."

The U.S. got within six when Brewer dunked a follow-up to a Dwight Jones miss. After Joyce dropped a pass while cutting through the lane, Sakandelidze took the ball all the way and dished to Aleksandr Belov for two, causing Gifford to mutter, almost to himself, about Sakandelidze, "Boy, he is fast." With the Soviet Union leading, 19-9, Russell noted the Americans had "made more offensive mistakes in this game than they have in the rest put together." With less than 10 minutes left in the first half, the U.S. had almost as many turnovers as points. Russell pointed the finger squarely at Iba, though not in so many words, saying, "They are not showing enough imagination on offense."

Jim Brewer didn't have much offensive imagination, but he did have heart, and he wasn't afraid to take a big shot. His outside jumper—"not really his shot," as Gifford diplomatically offered—swished home to draw the Americans within eight. Sergei Belov, though, was playing as if he would not let the Soviets lose. This time, he hit his feathery jumper from the right baseline, making it 21-11. Belov had 12 points on just seven shots.

In the last few minutes of the half, the U.S. at last took advantage of a lull in the Soviet offense as Sergei Belov cooled off a bit. A sharp pass from Bantom to a cutting Henderson resulted in a layup. Another Henderson lay-up made it 21-15. Baskets by Sakandelidze and Aleksandr Belov for the Soviets, and by Bantom, Henderson, and McMillen for the U.S. made the score at halftime 26-21. Bantom had committed his third foul just before halftime, and was the only U.S. player in foul trouble.

Things could have been much worse for the Americans than a five-point deficit. They finished the half with 10 turnovers to go with numerous juggled passes, bungled plays, and poor shots, some of which resulted in air balls. Each basket they scored seemed as difficult to come by as a touchdown in tackle football and was cause for nearly as much celebration. The Americans' fierce defense, though, was causing the Soviet offense to sputter as well, keeping the game close. But for Sergei Belov's torrid shooting, the U.S., even with all its problems on offense, might have led at the break.

For a Soviet squad that was the highest-scoring team in the tournament, 26 points at halftime was a shockingly low tally. The U.S. was doing a particularly good job on Aleksandr Belov, the big forward who had been a dominating force in the prior games, scoring 37 points in one of them. Iba wasn't much for halftime speeches, and during the break he went over the basics of what he felt the team needed to do better. Four times, the U.S. had beaten the Soviets in Olympics finals. If there was to be a fifth, Iba's prediction that summer to his coaches that the Soviets would collapse under the pressure of the tenacious U.S. defense would have to come true. Simply playing the Soviets to a draw in the second half would result in the first-ever

Olympic basketball loss for the seven-time defending champs.

The second half started much as the first had, with a string of turnovers and little scoring. With 15 minutes left, the Soviets led by six, 31-25. Henderson forced a shot that had no chance, as the Americans' offense became even more stagnant. The Soviet coaches had obviously scouted the U.S. team well, despite Iba's strategy of practicing during the Games at a CIA base miles outside Munich. At any one time, it appeared as if eight or nine Soviets were on the floor, filling every passing lane and swallowing up every rebound, thanks to Aleksandr Belov.

All the while, Iba sat quietly, albeit tensely, on the sideline. No strutting, screaming at the referees or the players, and no outraged leaps off of his chair. Bobby Knight he was not. If Iba was old-school when it came to his team's playing style and behavior on and off the court, he judged his own deportment by the same standard. If anything, according to his players, Iba was too passive, hewing to the deliberate offense that clearly wasn't working. "I felt like the coaches had put the reins on us," recalls Bobby Jones. "We really couldn't push it ahead and take a 3-on-2 or 2-on-1. I really felt that." The restrictive style that resulted in so few opportunities to score was becoming the main topic of discussion for Gifford and Russell in the broadcast booth. Gifford observed that "it must be frustrating for the players not to break out of this fixed style," to which Russell responded, "At this late stage, it might hurt more than it would help."

With the score 34-28 with 12 minutes left, a sequence of plays occurred that would cost the Americans two of their best big men and fuel conspiracy theories for years. Sergei Belov clanked a jumper off the rim and Dwight Jones and Mishako Korkia fought over the rebound. Like two kids in a playground, they wrestled over the ball even after the whistle had blown. The tape shows both players shoving each other hard as they were being disentangled. Dwight Jones stepped back and made a fist as one of the referees interjected. Immediately, the Brazilian referee, Renato Righetto, pointed at the two and threw up his thumbs, indicating the U.S.'s leading scorer was being thrown out of the game, along with the far less distinguished Korkia.

Although the referee clearly over-reacted, it's hard to say his actions were unfair. After all, he did throw both players out, Jones had shoved Korkia, and Jones had been caught in a fight stance with a cocked fist. The way Dwight Jones sees it, though, Korkia had one thing in mind. "I know he was sent in there to hit me," Jones recalled. "Hank Iba and everyone were going crazy. We were beginning to rebound and play better than we did in the first half and they stopped it."

Several years later, when Bantom was playing in Italy, some European players came up to him before one game and expressed disbelief that Jones had fallen for such a transparent ploy. Baiting one of the opposing team's best players was a standard tactic of Russian club basketball. On the other hand, however, Korkia was a starter, so it doesn't quite make sense that the Soviets would potentially sacrifice a starter to provoke Dwight Jones into overreacting.

Even before the U.S. team had fully comprehended that arguably its best player had been booted, the game resumed after the brouhaha with a jump ball. Brewer took the jump against Aleksandr Belov but lost his balance coming down, falling backward and banging his head on the court. U.S. Trainer Whitey Gwynne came out and looked Brewer over for several minutes. Although the contact wasn't as obvious as that involving Jones and Korkia, Brewer and many of his teammates believed his falling was no accident. Brewer maintains that Belov locked up his arms on purpose, causing him to lose his balance, and that another Soviet had tried the tactic earlier in the game. "That was definitely one of their little tricks off the jump ball," Brewer said. Brewer stayed in the game for the time being, but clearly looked shaken.

After still another Sergei Belov jump shot off a rebound, the Soviets led, 36-26, with just over 11 minutes remaining. The way the game was going, with Dwight Jones out and Brewer in a daze, a 10-point Soviet lead seemed as safe as a 20-point cushion under normal circumstances. The mostly pro-American crowd was hushed, the only real noise coming from one end of the court where some Soviet athletes from other sports had gathered to cheer on their countrymen. Gifford described a "stunned silence in the basketballhalle."

But after Ratleff converted a baseline floater and the dazed Brewer hit a jumper in traffic in front of the basket, the U.S. had pulled to within six, 36-30. The teams exchanged baskets for a couple of more precious minutes, the Americans unable to make any real dent in the lead. The Soviets led, 44-36,

8

with about five minutes left.

It was then that Kevin Joyce took charge. A native New Yorker and team leader who liked to tweak Iba, Joyce confronted the coach in a timeout huddle, saying they had to push the ball on offense and pressure the Soviets on defense. Joyce wasn't the only player who felt it was time to challenge the coaching staff. The players sensed the game slipping away and dreaded a legacy as the only U.S. team ever to lose a gold medal game in Olympic basketball—to the Soviets no less. "We all talked about it and said we have to put pressure on them," recalled Ratleff. "I remember we were saying, 'We have to go after them.'"

CHAPTER 2
The World Plays Catch-Up

That the Americans and Soviets met in the gold medal basketball game at the Munich Olympics shocked no one. Like a specter on the horizon, the matchup could be seen approaching years before.

On the strength of its gold medal win in Mexico City in 1968, the United States entered the '72 Olympics having won seven consecutive gold medals in basketball. The streak stretched all the way back to the first Olympic basketball competition, at the 1936 Summer Games in Berlin, where the contests were played on a muddy outdoor court and the scores hovered in the 20s and the mid-teens. A good indication of where the U.S. national basketball team stood then in relation to the rest of the world in 1936 was that the Americans beat host Germany, 130-8, in what was no doubt intended to be humiliating put-down of the Nazi regime.

Thirty-six years later, the U.S. still had a far deeper talent pool from which to select a national team than any other country, and that wasn't even including stars of the professional game, such as Oscar Robertson, Kareem Abdul-Jabbar, Jerry West, Walt Frazier, Bill Bradley, Rick Barry and John Havlicek. Eligible collegiate stars heading into the 1971-72 season included Julius Erving, Bill Walton, George McGinnis, David Thompson, Marvin Barnes, Larry Kenon, Ed Ratleff, Tom McMillen and Dwight Jones.

The impressive U.S. talent notwithstanding, the air of invincibility surrounding the national team had been eroding ever so slightly since the Americans' comfortable 15-point victory over Yugoslavia in the 1968 gold medal game. In May 1970, the Americans lost a rematch with the Yugoslavs, 70-63, in the semifinals of the World Basketball Championships, as a young Bill Walton made his one and only appearance representing his country. That same year, the U.S. suffered its first-ever loss in the World University Games, a 78-71 defeat to the Soviets. While few viewed that result as an omen of things to come, the very next year the U.S. lost its first game of the

1971 Pan American Games, to Cuba in Cali, Colombia, breaking a 24-game unbeaten streak in Pan Am competition and losing a place in the medal round. The fact that the entire U.S. team had been crammed into a small, filthy barracks that lacked proper window screens was part of the deal when it came to international competition. In other words, there was no explaining away the Americans' embarrassing performance.

As for the Soviets, their one-point loss to the Yugoslavs in the 1968 Olympic semifinal game could easily be dismissed as a fluke. Coming into the game, the Soviets had won all of their contests in Mexico City by an average of 25 points. Their missed opportunity to play the Americans for the gold served only to make the Soviets hungrier for victory in Munich four years later.

Throughout the late 1960s and early '70s, in fact, Soviet players' skills became more sophisticated, their domestic league grew stronger and the country's results in international competition improved. The Cold War imperative of beating the United States at its native game made basketball one of the top priorities in Soviet sports. To that end, the core of the Soviet Red Army team was kept constant year after year; the team played hundreds of games together between 1968 and 1972. The roster that beat the Americans in the 1970 World University Games, for example, included most of the same players who would compete in the 1972 Olympics, including stars Aleksandr Belov and Sergei Belov (who, despite their shared surname, were unrelated).

Since the Soviets had started competing in international basketball in the 1952 Helsinki Games, they had won the European Championship 11 times. In 1967, led by Sergei Belov, the Soviets won the World Championships. As for the Olympics, Soviet teams had played the bridesmaid to the U.S. four times, taking the silver in 1952, 1956, 1960 and 1964. Even in 1952, the Soviets had demonstrated savvy gamesmanship, freezing the ball for minutes at a time in the gold medal game against the United States before eventually succumbing, 36-25.

Besides the Soviet Union, Yugoslavia and Cuba, the national basketball programs in Brazil, Spain and Italy also had made major strides by 1972. The U.S. itself was responsible for much of this surge in international talent, having sent coaches and players abroad as basketball ambassadors to teach the finer points of the game. In 1969, a group of collegiate all-stars—including a guard named Kenny Davis, who would end up making the 1972 Olympic squad—played a goodwill exhibition tour in Africa and Europe. The tour included several games behind the Iron Curtain in Poland and Czechoslovakia. Another example of how Americans had fostered the game was that the Puerto Rico national team at Munich was coached by then-Memphis State coach Gene Bartow, as an extension of his significant basketball outreach on the island. If there was a nation improving its basketball, often there was an American involved in the effort.

Even some of the actors involved in the 1972 game had played a hand in improving the Soviet team. Johnny Bach, an assistant coach on the 1972 team who coached Penn State at the time, had traveled to the Soviet Union to conduct clinics in the late 1960s. "Any city I went to," Bach recalled, "they had only one reel of someone shooting—Jerry West. Who was the best jump shooter of all time? Jerry West. You could see that the Russians were coming."

Bach's fears came true in the spring of 1971 when he took an Olympic development team of collegians, including Tom McMillen, then a freshman at Maryland, to Russia, Poland and Finland. What Bach saw opened his eyes even wider. "The Soviets' jump shooting, passing, the crispness of what they do is amazing—and alarming," Bach told the *Washington Post* at the time. "Their defense is especially admirable, aggressive with great individual responsibility." Later that year, as one of the coaches of the 1971 Pan American team that lost to Cuba in the opening round, Bach again could see up close just how much international rivals to U.S. dominance were on the rise.

Not everyone, however, bought into the idea of Americans' acting as missionaries for the game. Lefty Driesell, the famed University of Maryland coach who mentored McMillen for four years, made a point of never doing ambassadorial work overseas. "I was invited a lot of times to go to Europe and give clinics," Driesell said. "And I said, 'What would I want to teach them for?' The Russians were very good. They were physical. They were strong. They could shoot. There were people here in America that needed to learn how to play basketball."

Few people involved in the game, however, shared that view. Many U.S. coaches seemed to understand that, while the rest of the world's improvement in basketball may have posed a challenge to the United States' historical dominance of the sport, such a development actually was good for all involved. For one thing, it pushed the Americans to get better. Perhaps more important was the signal that it sent. The rise of other basketball nations, with a helping hand from the U.S., marked a major cultural victory for the United States. Here were Eastern Bloc nations (and others) embracing a sport founded in the United States and managing to credibly compete in it on an international stage. As Carson Cunningham wrote in his book *American Hoops: U.S. Men's Olympic Basketball from Berlin to Beijing:* "The rise of international sports, basketball in particular, was facilitating cultural exchanges and promoting a common desire for Western products. This was suggested by the Soviet and Yugoslav coaches' ready admission that they had borrowed heavily from American basketball style."

CHAPTER 3
The Legend as Coach

The first issue for USA Basketball concerning the 1972 Olympic team was what to do about Hank Iba. After Mexico City, Iba had hinted to confidantes and the Basketball Federation of the United States of America that he wasn't particularly interested in pushing his luck by trying for a third gold medal. His son, the former Nebraska Cornhusker Coach Moe Iba, would later confirm that his father had no intentions of coaching the 1972 team.

But Iba was a living legend, and therefore his name always remained in the discussion. After two seasons as a high school coach, Iba became the head coach at Oklahoma A&M—later renamed Oklahoma State—in 1934. From the mid-1930s to the early 1950s, Iba fielded 19 consecutive winning teams and won two national titles, all in his trademark style. In the 1945 national championship game, Oklahoma A&M beat NYU, 49-45. Iba's team successfully defended its title the next year by beating North Carolina, 43-40. Iba returned to the finals one more time, in 1949, only this time his team lost, 46-36, to Kentucky and its famed coach Adolph Rupp. Those results eventually earned Iba his first Olympic coaching position, at the Tokyo Games in 1964. After winning the gold medal there, he became the obvious choice to coach the U.S. team in Mexico City in 1968.

To describe Iba as being an old-school coach is putting it mildly. Iba's father successfully managed a series of barnstorming semipro baseball teams, a job that exposed his son to the discipline, organization and camaraderie needed to fuse a team of otherwise disparate players. Iba was further influenced in how young college men should behave by his fraternity experience at Westminster College in Missouri, because the fraternity life removed, as he put it, "carelessness and selfishness" from his life. Iba was quoted in 1972 by an Oklahoma State alumni publication as saying the initial questions he would ask a player were about his family background.

"[T]he first thing I would like to know is: how much discipline was in the home? I then like to go to his high school and find his scholastic background, his class attendance and his ability to get along with people. Then, of course, one must look at a man's physical attributes, such as strength, speed, and body movement, but that's the last thing to look for."

Ironically enough, for a coach who would go on to win two gold medals, Iba's approach to the game was rooted in identifying with the underdog. Iba, throughout his career, would often point to one game that helped him forge his basketball philosophy. Iba was travelling with a barnstorming team that was playing a game at a homecoming of soldiers from World War I in the small town of Stewardsville, Missouri. Badly outmanned, his team lost, 62-14. On the way home, Iba began to conceive of methods of coaching, both offensive and defensive, that could enable an overpowered team to dictate the flow of a game.

The strategy he came up with was simple but brutally effective: an in-your-face defense coupled with a patient offense based on passing, moving without the ball and shooting only when an open shot arose. According to his obituary in the *New York Times,* Iba would begin each collegiate season by repeating this mantra to his players: "We're not going to play them; they're going to play us." In a 2004 dissertation on the Munich Games, the historian Christopher Elzey recounted a story published in the *Nashville Banner* in 1972. "During Iba's younger days as a coach, he would often let his players drive the team van to and from road games. Once, coming back after a tough defeat, the player at the wheel noticed that the van was almost out of gas. 'Coach,' the young player said, 'we need gas.' Iba snapped, 'You just do the driving. I'll tell you when we need gas.' Before long, the engine quit, the gas tank empty. Iba finally said, 'Okay, boys, I'm going to drive. The rest of you get out and push.'"

Although Iba was a taskmaster on the court, his success in the NCAA championship and the Olympics never affected his humble persona. Coach Bobby Knight described his first meeting with Iba, at a recruiting event at the Akron Touchdown Club's Basketball banquet sometime in the late 1960s. Knight was standing near Iba when the veteran coach turned to him and said, "Son, my name is Henry Iba." To which Knight replied, "Coach, I've known who you are since I first started playing basketball." Iba went on to compliment Knight's work on defense with his Army team at West Point. "When he walked in a room, you knew he was somebody," Knight said. "He had a tremendous presence. There isn't a coach since 1940 that doesn't do something Henry Iba initiated, and most of them don't know where it came from."

The beauty of Iba's style early on at Oklahoma State was that it took great advantage of the rules of the day. In the 1940s and '50s, there was no shot clock in the college (or pro) game to limit how long a team could retain possession of the ball. The rules would stay that way until the 24-second shot clock was invented by the owner of the Syracuse Nationals (later the Philadelphia 76ers) in 1956 when he and other owners had grown tired of seeing fans leave in droves in the last few minutes of games, as players like the Celtics' Bob Cousy iced the game by simply dribbling out the final few minutes. Later, the college game would adopt a 45-second, and, eventually, today's 30-second shot clock.

Another of Iba's idiosyncrasies was that he refused to rank the best players of his era above any others. For example, even though his Oklahoma State team faced off against Wilt Chamberlain many times when Chamberlain played for the University of Kansas, Iba would never answer directly when asked how Chamberlain stacked up in terms of Oklahoma State's historically toughest opponents. Instead, Iba cited the skills of other players, such as Byron (Whizzer) White, a football standout who also played basketball at the University of Colorado (and would later become a Supreme Court justice). Critics of Iba said his tendency to downplay the role of scorers and stars seeped into the way he coached, and that Iba's teams inevitably left lots of easy points on the floor.

One might assume that a philosophy rooted in self-sacrifice, discipline and family background—not to mention strict shot selection—would have left Iba ill-equipped to coach college players in the 1960s, when athletes were not immune from the student movements rippling across the country. But his two successive national championships at Oklahoma State and two Olympic gold medals made Iba one of the most decorated basketball coaches in the country. He couldn't be eliminated from the 1972 Olympic search quite so easily, even though he didn't actually want the assignment.

After all, as far as the U.S. Olympic Basketball Committee was concerned, Iba's experience might come in handy in a year when any coach would face challenges bringing home a gold medal, given the state of the amateur game in America. In contrast to the Soviets' single-minded, collective devotion to wresting Olympic basketball glory away from the United States, the U.S. national basketball program by 1972 had become a revolving door of players. Many of them played just one event and never donned the uniform of the stars and stripes again. The United States essentially reinvented its international basketball team for every tournament, forging a squad over a week or so of tryouts, breaking it up after the tournament and then selecting a new team for the next event.

For example, at the 1970 World Basketball Championships, Bill Walton was the only marquee player on the U.S. team, but he never played again for the country. Walton's team did not include future Hall of Famer George McGinnis or Marquette star Jim Chones, both of whom played that same year for America at the World University Games. Future NBA greats Paul Westphal and Bob McAdoo played on neither of these teams, though they did suit up for the Pan American Games in 1971. That Pan Am team had just three players in common with the roster that would play in Munich the next year. "There was no continuity in the program," recalled Doug Collins, who was a key guard on the 1972 Olympic team and now coaches the NBA's Philadelphia 76ers. "It used to be that you had the Pan American Games and the World Championships and then the Olympics, so guys played three years together before making the Olympic team. Guys had played together and had gained international experience." But then, Collins added, "guys started leaving early to go to the pros, so all of a sudden Julius Erving and all these great players were going to the NBA, and there was no continuity. I think we had a total of seven games of international experience on our 1972 Olympic team."

CHAPTER 4

The Siren Song of the Professional Game

What was at the root of the discontinuous nature of the U.S. basketball program? Collins gets it exactly right when he cites the encroachment of the professional game. By 1972, the NBA and the American Basketball Association—the league of the red, white and blue ball that kids everywhere twirled in the early '70s—were bidding against each other for the best college players. The battle for talent accelerated the signing process, spurring teams to pursue players almost as soon as—sometimes even before—the last game of the college season. What's more, the ABA had no restrictions against signing undergraduates. Both Erving, the technical and spiritual predecessor of Michael Jordan, and George McGinnis, a future perennial all-star, were signed by the ABA in the spring of 1972 before they had exhausted their NCAA eligibility, meaning that as pros they could not play in the Olympics.

To indicate just how much the ABA had changed players' calculus about going pro versus staying in college and retaining their amateur status, one need look no further than Jim Chones, the starting center for then-undefeated Marquette University, who leapt at the opportunity to sign with the New York Nets *with six games remaining* in the 1971-72 collegiate season. Long before the term March Madness had been coined, the phrase could be used to describe the fierce recruitment of players by the ABA every spring in the early 1970s. The upstart league was at the height of its influence then. No one expected the ABA would be defunct by 1976, when four of its teams merged with the NBA. The ABA and its big bucks were powerful draws for many college players who, despite being well-known stars, did not have money to take their dates out to dinner on Saturday night.

Founded in 1967, the ABA at first offered too little money to really affect the NBA draft. Upon graduating from UCLA in 1969, Kareem Abdul-

18

Jabbar (who at the time still went by his birth name, Lew Alcindor) flew to New York for a meeting with the ABA's New York Nets. Abdul-Jabbar, a New York native, was ready to opt for the new league for the right offer, particularly since he had little interest in playing for the Milwaukee Bucks, the NBA team that held his rights. But the Nets' offer proved too little for him to be swayed from taking the tried-and-true route of the NBA. The fledgling league lost out on a player who would have been a defining attraction.

But as the years went by, ABA officials learned that they could exploit two advantages over its far more established rival. Not only did the ABA have no restrictions on signing college players before graduation (or, as in the case of Chones, even during the season), there was an unwritten rule among the NBA, the NCAA and the AAU that NBA teams, in Olympic years, would wait to sign graduating players until after the Games. The ABA, on the other hand, played by no such gentlemanly rules. It used its dollars and aggressiveness to sign such stars as Erving, McGinnis, Moses Malone, Billy Cunningham, Artis Gilmore, George Gervin, Dan Issel, Rick Barry and Roger Brown.

The ABA's policies and tactics diminshed the pool of available Olympic talent. Although nothing was guaranteed for any player who tried out for the Olympic team in 1972, Erving, Chones and McGinnis—to name only three—each possessed the skill and maturity that would have made him an excellent candidate for the team. Several players who ended up on the 1972 Olympic team had been approached by the ABA but decided to stay in college, motivated partly by a desire to play in the Olympics. Ed Ratleff, for instance, was approached by the Denver Nuggets, Indiana Pacers and Miami Floridians after his junior year. "They all tried to get me to go, and I did talk to them," Ratleff recalled, "but I decided to stay." The ABA's aggressive recruiting wasn't limited to players. By 1969, the league even was recruiting officials. Veteran referee Norm Drucker jumped to the ABA along with fellow refs Joe Gushue, John Vanak and Earl Strom. Their lure: $50,000 salaries plus signing bonuses, according to Charles Salzberg's oral history *From Set Shot to Slam Dunk*.

By late 1971, even the NBA started getting in on the act. In a case brought by Spencer Haywood, a high-scorer who would go on to have a strong NBA career with several teams, a Los Angeles District Court judge struck down the restriction on NBA players signing underclassmen. In response, the NBA came up with the concept of "hardship cases"—underclassmen who were allowed to enter the draft because their families were in financial straits. Conspiracy theorists will note that the Los Angeles judge's ruling would, eight years later, bring Earvin "Magic" Johnson to the Los Angeles Lakers.

Following the failure of the United States team to make the medal round at the 1971 Pan Am Games, Herb Mols, manager of the national basketball program, wrote in a publication of the U.S. Olympic Committee in December 1971 that troubles stemmed from the "the inroads of professional sports in the U.S." Mols added: "Perhaps now our admonitions of the past several years will be accepted for what they are worth. We must be realistic in our understanding of the growth of basketball abroad. We are acutely aware of the drain of our top resources into professional ranks. HOW DO WE ADDRESS THIS CHALLENGE?"

Besides players' entering the professional ranks, there was another major reason the U.S. team was often left short-handed for international tournaments. The rising power of the NCAA was increasingly diminishing the status of the Amateur Athletic Union. The governing body of amateur sports in the United States, the AAU traditionally fielded industrial and military basketball teams, and thus supplied older players who had international experience to the Olympics and similar competitions. Difficult as it is to imagine today, a half-century ago some of the top amateur players in the country were playing for military or corporate-affiliated teams sponsored by the AAU, such as the Goodyear Wingfoots of Akron, Ohio, and the Phillips 66ers of Bartlesville, Oklahoma.

For years, especially in the 1930s and 1940s, the AAU was the choice for former college players who, for one reason or another, weren't playing in the pros but still were at the top of their games. For instance, in *From Set Shot to Slam Dunk,* George "The Bird" Yardley, one of the game's great leapers in the 1950s, explained why he opted to play in the AAU for three years after graduating from Stanford, even though professional teams beckoned. "One year I was with Stewart Chevrolet and we won the national championship and I was named MVP of the AAU," Yardley said. "I was desperate to play in the Olympics." In 1952, USA Basketball allotted six spots for the

NCAA and six spots for the AAU, indicating how at the time the AAU stood on equal footing with the NCAA in terms of amateur basketball. Players such as Yardley joined AAU teams so they could keep playing competitive basketball while retaining their Olympic eligibility.

Vestiges of this system remained in place in 1972. Kenny Davis had graduated from Georgetown College in Kentucky and was playing for the AAU's Marathon Oil team when he was selected to join the Olympic team that would compete in Munich. But the diminished stature of the AAU in basketball resulted in lack of experienced veterans of international basketball. The resulting hard feelings damaged the selection process even more, as AAU officials clung to their power and could block the selection of some collegiate players at the various tryout camps. "For the longest time, the AAU had been in charge of the players who went to the Olympics," Davis said. "Obviously, as time progressed the NCAA had the better players. So there was a feud at the time between the NCAA and the AAU about who was in control. Even though the AAU only had one player spot, if you look at the trainers and the staff at the time, they were all still AAU people."

The coaches of the 1972 Olympic team knew that, given the advancing basketball skills of other nations and the stacked deck against the amateur game in the U.S., victory in Munich was not assured. "If the pros sign all the boys we'd like, and they seem determined to do so, we are going to have to scramble to keep competitive," Hank Iba told the *Washington Post*. "We can't survive this situation."

CHAPTER 5

The King and Crown Prince of College Basketball

Besides the siren song of the pros and the subsequent loss of influence on the part of the AAU, by the spring of 1972 there was another reason the U.S. Olympic team would be short-handed: the conspicuous absence of Bill Walton. UCLA was at the epicenter of college basketball. The Bruins' coach, John Wooden, was the king, and Walton the crown prince.

Of all the players eligible for the Olympic team, it was Walton, UCLA's star center and the most dominant collegiate player of the day, whom U.S. national team observers were watching the closest. To see Walton play in the pivot in the 1970s, both at UCLA and later with the NBA's Portland Trailblazers, was to witness a position being reinvented.

Not many basketball players can claim to have redefined the sport. In later years, Los Angeles Lakers point guard Magic Johnson would join Walton as someone who had the skills, size and basketball intelligence to re-imagine his position. (Even as great he was, Michael Jordan was simply the best-ever scoring guard; it's difficult to argue that he changed the nature of the position.) As Hall of Famer Jerry West said in Salzberg's *From Set Shot to Slam Dunk*, "Basketball is a relatively young game, and every time you have a great star, someone who improves on something, you'll have another kid come along who improves on that."

In Walton's case, he played center not simply as the big man who received the ball in the post but instead as a "point center" of sorts, deftly passing, moving without the ball and choosing from his portfolio of highly polished scoring moves. During one NCAA tournament game, Walton made 21 of 22 shots in one of the most dominant and precise performances in basketball history. In that game Walton was guarded by Larry Kenon, who would be cut from the 1972 trials in Colorado Springs but go on to become a standout pro. It didn't matter what Kenon tried on defense; there simply was no stopping Walton when he was at his best—he was too big and too skilled to be denied. As Ed Ratleff, a member of the 1972 Olympic team, recalled: "Walton was an incredible player. No one could guard him." Concurred Doug Collins: "If we had Bill Walton, it would have been a different ballgame because he was by far the most dominant college player."

It was neither professional dollars nor basketball politics that kept Walton off the team. Walton's announcement that he wouldn't be joining the Olympic team came after the 1971-72 UCLA season ended, when a doctor diagnosed the basketball star with tendonitis in both knees and recommended rest until the following college basketball season. When it came to Bill Walton, though, there was usually more to a situation than met the eye. "With Bill, we would have had the most dominant player in the Olympics, by far," recalled Johnny Bach. "But Bill was mad about the war or something."

At the time of the Munich Olympics, Walton was in the middle of an absurd streak of five straight years—from the middle of his junior year in high school to the middle of his senior year at UCLA—when whatever team he was playing on did not lose a single game. It's highly unlikely that Walton's streak would have been interrupted by the likes of the Soviets, whose most effective big man, Aleksandr Belov, was six inches shorter than Walton, who was typically listed at 6-foot-11 (but is generally recognized to have been 7-2). Eventually, Walton would be named the top college basketball player in the country for three consecutive years in 1972, 1973, and 1974. As Kenny Davis put it: "Walton would have made a big difference and the final game wouldn't have been that close if Olympic officials could have done anything for him."

The question remains, 40 years later: What exactly did Walton want "done for him"? For his part, Walton's UCLA teammate Swen Nater believes Walton's decision to skip the Olympics might have been a case of Walton's being, well, Bill Walton. He was first and foremost a child of the West Coast. Since enrolling at UCLA, Walton had embraced a countercultural ethos. He ate only organic foods and expounded on the platforms of free speech and protest. Walton, in fact, was one of the few big-time college athletes who were active in the antiwar movement, and by far the most famous. Although he didn't come out and say he was boycotting the 1972 Summer Olympics as a protest of the Vietnam War, it certainly wasn't clear that the war *didn't* have anything to do with his sitting out the Olympics. "Bill was not one to play summer ball," Nater said. "He liked to get away from the game a little bit. Bill liked to hike and eat berries and whatever else he was into."

Also, to be fair, Walton was in constant knee, foot and ankle pain throughout his entire career, and it had already started in college. He would later earn the dubious distinction of missing more games, on a per season average, than any player in NBA history. But the very fact of his ubiquitous injuries also meant that Walton often played through pain, and many believe his decision to skip the Munich games was more tied to his own, and to UCLA's, resentment of the national basketball program.

What's never been unearthed before, however, is that, according to Bobby Knight, there existed a tacit understanding that Walton, if his knees and feet felt good enough, could board the plane leaving from Washington, D.C., for Munich just for the Games—without having to endure the grind of tryouts, training camp and preliminary games against the teams of NBA players. "It was my understanding that Walton had a free ticket to play on the team," Knight said. Johnny Bach and several players also said Walton would have been welcome at the last minute, perhaps by everyone except Coach Iba.

Part of the collective willingness to make exceptions for Walton was grounded in the dawning realization that the Americans were likely to face a reckoning in their probable gold medal game matchup with the Soviets. That's why Walton's dominance in the middle was so important to the U.S. plans, and why, when interviewed nearly 40 years later, Knight was still angry about Walton's decision not to play. "Guys that have a chance to play for their country, you know, they've done a little bit more in sports than guys that have been just great players," Knight said. "I don't have any use for Walton. He knows it and I know it. He was not incapacitated. He just didn't want to go." The closest the 1972 team came to landing Walton was the selection of Nater, Walton's backup at UCLA, who made the team only to quit a few days into the gruelling training camp at Pearl Harbor.

Walton may have been reluctant to play in the Olympics because of his previous experience in international competition and the militaristic approach to the 1972 Games that would surely be coming if Iba was named coach. As a callow 17-year-old, Walton had been a member of the U.S. Armed Forces team, run by the AAU, that played in the World Championships in Yugoslavia. Walton was the only player on the team who was not in the Army. In his 1994 autobiography, Walton wrote that one of his coaches there was "the most abusive man I had ever met in my life." According to Walton's book, one message this coach was fond of delivering was that for those players who didn't make the team, "I'm going to personally sign your orders for combat duty in Vietnam." Several of those players who failed to get picked for the team, he wrote, did, in fact, end up fighting in the jungles of Indochina.

According to Bill Wall, an executive with the U.S. Olympic Basketball Committee at the time, the head coach of the U.S. team at that World Championships, Hal Fisher, treated Walton "like a dog." "He may have been the youngest kid on the team, and we had some renegades in that group who were basically playing basketball to avoid going to Vietnam," Wall said.

Although the team went undefeated, the Americans failed to qualify for the medal round because the differential of their victories was so slim. They finished in fifth place, no small embarrassment. It was the first and last time Walton would ever play for a U.S. national team. The experience dissuaded Walton from taking the U.S. Olympic Basketball Committee up on their feelers that he play on the 1972 team. According to Walton, he told the "suits" that he did not intend to drop out of UCLA at any point to make himself available for the Munich Games, or go through any "boot-camp tryout session." "If they wanted me to live in Army barracks, sleep in tiny beds, eat at mess halls and play in a bunch of meaningless exhibition games," he wrote in his autobiography. "I wasn't interested." Knowing how the World Championships experience might be playing a part in Walton's reluctance to play, Wall at one point approached Walton and asked him directly if he would play. Walton responded with a simple no.

Yet another potential factor in Walton's not playing on the team was the famously frigid relationship that UCLA Coach John Wooden had with the committee that selected the U.S. basketball coach. Despite his long tenure at UCLA and numerous NCAA championships, Wooden had never been approached to coach the national team.

The unspoken etiquette in those days was that college coaches had to make it known they were interested in the Olympic job. Iba, a patriot to the core, had no problem stepping forward in that manner. According to several people, Wooden figured that, with his litany of accomplishments, anyone who wanted to talk to him about coaching in the Olympics should approach *him*. "I think some people thought they were above throwing their hat in the ring at a certain point in their career," said Johnny Bach, one of the two assistants on the '72 Olympic team. Although Wooden's proud stance may make sense to outside observers, anyone who understood the politics of Olympic basketball at the time knew things didn't work the way he hoped they would.

The late Gene Bartow, who coached the Puerto Rican team during the 1972 Olympics and later succeeded Wooden as the head coach at UCLA, believed Wooden chose not to pursue the chance to lead the U.S. for different reasons. The Olympics, Bartow once said, weren't Wooden's "cup of tea." "I'm sure he had many chances to coach a lot of different national teams or whatever over the years," Bartow said. "I just think he battled so hard during the year that he didn't want to take on a national team responsibility." Wooden himself was quoted in a biography about him, *The Wizard of Westwood,* as saying that he felt the spirit of the Games had changed. "It has become more political," he said, adding that "the kids just don't have the desire any more." All the average person cared about in terms of the Olympics, Wooden said, was how the U.S. was going to fare against Russia. "Is that what the Olympics are about?" he said. "Are we participating against just one team, or are we participating against all countries? I'm as patriotic as anyone, but I've become disillusioned" with the Olympics.

It is not hard to see why Wooden may have been put off by the need for him to lobby his case for the Olympic coaching job. By 1972, Wooden had put together an unprecedented track record at UCLA, all with an avuncular, studious style that was respected by fans, university administrators, and players alike. Wooden's dual success at winning basketball championships and seeing to it that his players graduated was particularly impressive given the tumult of the era, when the Vietnam War was stoking student protests on campuses around the country and tragedies like the shootings at Kent State led collegiate players to question authority as never before.

In contrast to all the unrest, there was nothing simpler than a 40-minute basketball game with a clear winner and loser—that is, before the 1972 Olympic gold medal game—and no coach was better at producing victories than Wooden. In fact, according to a 2004 dissertation on the Munich Games by historian Christopher Clark Elzey, thousands of fans from all walks of life would write to Wooden, asking for a copy of or insights from his *Pyramid of Success*, a book in which Wooden spelled out his leadership philosophy. A college admissions director wrote to say that he'd hung a poster of the coach's diagrammed pyramid of "building blocks" (*industriousness, friendship, loyalty...*) and made it the credo of the admissions office. Business leaders did the same. The vice president of one corporation marveled at how the *Pyramid of Success* served as "a one-page condensation of any three books on management."

Whatever the reasons, Wooden didn't coach the United States Olympic basketball team in 1972 and Walton didn't play on it. UCLA's indifference towards the Olympics wouldn't have been such a big deal had the absolute apex of the UCLA dynasty not coincided with the Munich Summer Games. During the 1971-72 season, the Bruins had won the NCAA Championship for the sixth year in a row, and the eighth time in the previous nine years. But, in fact, the relationship between UCLA basketball and the Olympics had long had a chicken-and-the-egg quality about it. Which came first: UCLA's lack of enthusiasm for Olympic basketball, or Olympic basketball's slights toward UCLA. An apparent snubbing of Bruins center Willie Naulls in 1956 may have been one of the triggers of tensions between UCLA and Olympics officials. Naulls scored 42 points over three Olympic trial games, and was the third-leading rebounder at the 1956 trials, but still was cut from the team. Despite UCLA's winning eight national championships under Wooden as of 1972 (he would go on to win two more as well), only a single UCLA player—Walt Hazzard—had been chosen for an Olympic team until Swen Nater gained a spot in '72.

CHAPTER 6
Politics and Basketball Intersect

It is also worth noting that, like Walton, Kareem Abdul-Jabbar had also passed on trying out for the Olympic team four years earlier. Abdul-Jabbar's decision was rooted more in his dawning realization of just how far blacks had to go in America to achieve racial equality. Stories like the one of how Cassius Clay had won a gold medal in the 1960 Olympics in Rome only to be refused service in a restaurant in the South—while wearing the medal around his neck—affected Abdul-Jabbar deeply.

During the Olympic summer of 1968, the UCLA star changed his name to the Muslim moniker by which he remains known today. In his autobiography, *Giant Steps*, Abdul-Jabbar wrote about the feelings he had at the time toward his country and the Olympics. "If white America was going to treat blacks poorly, then white America could win the Olympics on its own," he wrote. "We all felt the effects of racial prejudice, from individual hurtful remarks to difficulties getting decent housing or good jobs." He said he "fully supported" the idea of a boycott and "felt no part of the country and had no desire to help it look good."

Ultimately, there was no official boycott by black athletes of the 1968 Summer Games, but many, like Abdul-Jabbar, would personally chose not to participate. Interestingly, Abdul-Jabbar didn't mention whether or not Wooden encouraged or discouraged him from playing in the Olympics. But Abdul-Jabbar did note in his book that, watching the Games on television that summer, he was "fiercely proud" of John Carlos and Tommie Smith, the two U.S. track stars who made a controversial political statement by thrusting their black-gloved fists into the air on the medal stand as a display of black power. "My passive gesture had cost me a lot," Abdul-Jabbar wrote. "I was deluged by hate mail calling me an uppity nigger and a traitor, and I knew their active statement, in the public eye of that hurricane, would cost them much more. I think of them as patriots." Iba's team won the gold in Mexico

City without Abdul-Jabbar, who spent the summer teaching basketball to children in clinics sponsored by the New York City Housing Authority.

Although many in the media and on the UCLA campus called for Wooden to kick Abdul-Jabbar off the team for his refusing to try out for the Olympics, Wooden did no such thing. Besides Wooden's already frosty relationship with the powers that be in U.S. Olympic basketball circles, the coach also knew that had Abdul-Jabbar played in the Olympics, it would come at a cost to the UCLA team. He would have had to miss a quarter of the school year, and therefore be ineligible for the first nine games on the UCLA schedule and, more important to Wooden, fail to graduate on time. As with Walton four years later, it is unclear which factors figured most heavily in Abdul-Jabbar's decision not to play in the Olympic Games: macro events (the proposed boycott), personal circumstances (missing school), and or the lack of enthusiasm for the Olympics on the part of UCLA.

The Black Power movement that Abdul-Jabbar mentioned in his autobiography and that led to the Carlos/Smith medal stand salute in 1968 was closely watched by U.S. basketball officials going into the 1972 Olympics. More than one source said that iconic demonstration, as well as student protests on campuses around the nation, had basketball officials concerned about the possibility of a similar incident taking place in Munich.

CHAPTER 7

Meanwhile, Back in the Soviet Union

But it wasn't student unrest or a boycott by black athletes that U.S. basketball officials should have feared most as they prepared for the 1972 Summer Games.

There was more and more evidence mounting that, whatever the makeup of the final U.S. team, the Soviets would be tough to beat. In the spring of 1971, the Soviet national team traveled to America to play a series of games against teams of American collegiate all-stars. Facing teams with such future NBA and ABA stars as Erving, McGinnis, Gilmore and Randy Smith, the Soviets finished the tour with an impressive 9-1 record. Of the 12 Soviet players who competed on that tour, seven would be on the Olympic roster a year later in Munich.

The Soviets' best player was Sergei Belov, a sure-handed 6-foot-3 guard. Belov would eventually be the first European player to be inducted into the Naismith Basketball Hall of Fame. Another perimeter player was Modestas Paulauskas, 27, a swingman who had been one the Soviets' stars on their 1971 tour. Aleksandr Belov (no relation to Segei), a 6-8 forward with the physique and vertical leap of a top-flight NBA player, drew comparisons to Bernard King and was deemed by many to be the best athlete on the Soviet team. Both Belovs had played on the '71 tour, as did inside players such as Alshan Sharmukhamedov, a 6-9 center who was the team's best rebounder, and the 7-1 Sergei Kovalenko.

Curiously, U.S. basketball officials never really scouted the Soviets. The consensus seemed to be that, even though the Soviets were clearly a team to be reckoned with, any decent U.S. squad would be good enough to win the gold. The specific strengths and weaknesses of individual Soviet players, this thinking went, wouldn't change that inevitable outcome.

But some research into the Soviet system would have served the Americans well. Knowing the different places within the Soviet Union that each player came from might have helped the Americans understand how each Soviet would play as an individual. As Carson Cunningham wrote in his book *American Hoops: U.S. Men's Olympic Basketball from Berlin to Beijing*, "Players from the Baltic republics tended to be the best technicians while players from the Russian republic relied more on their athleticism." By contrast, ballplayers from the southern Soviet republics, especially Georgia, tended to create more than their teammates from the north did. Cunningham concluded that the Soviets' overall style of play was a mix.

But the Soviets certainly ran when they got the chance. Of the 16 teams in the 1972 Olympic basketball tournament, the Soviets averaged the highest number of points per game (91). The United States ranked fifth, at 77 points per game. In fact, the Americans' ability to hold the Soviets to 41 points below their Olympic average in the gold medal game provides support to Johnny Bach's contention for 40 years now that the Soviets would have scored a lot more had the U.S. picked up the pace of the game.

Any discussion of the rapid improvement in Soviet basketball during this period isn't complete, however, without addressing the hypocrisy surrounding amateurism in sports. Although the NCAA had its own problems enforcing its amateur status rules, with deep-pocketed alumni forging close relationships with collegiate players, the professionalization with which the Soviets pursued Olympic glory in not just basketball but all sports was well-known to Avery Brundage, head of the International Olympic Committee.

According to a 1993 article in *Olympika: The International Journal of Olympic Studies,* prominent Soviet athletes were deemed "Masters of Sport"—in effect, professional athletes. Masters of Sport received lifetime appointments as officers in the Soviet armed forces, "studentships" for as long as their athletic careers lasted, or—like a character from the HBO series *The Sopranos*—factory jobs to which they needn't show up. "In today's condition of *glasnost* and beyond, all of this is admitted in the USSR," the article asserted. But in 1972, Brundage took the standard line that, unless caught red-handed, claims by the Soviet Union and other Eastern Bloc countries that they were following Olympic rules to the letter had to be accepted at face value. At one point in the mid-1950s, Brundage wrote to his fellow IOC members that, "It is difficult, of course, under present conditions to tell what takes place behind the Iron Curtain," but that the committee should accept the Soviets' declaration of amateurism "and assume that the Olympic rules are being followed until we learn to the contrary."

But, as the *Olympika* article pointed out, it was many years before information "to the contrary" came to light. By the late 1980s, the Soviet Union had become the most decorated sporting nation in the world, having won more Olympic medals than any other nation since the Soviets' debut in Helsinki in 1952. Even East Germany, with approximately 17 million citizens at the time, won more gold medals in the Summer Games than the United States did in both 1976 and 1988.

CHAPTER 8
Now Wanted: A Coach

By early 1971, the coaching issue needed to be resolved. According to Bill Wall of the selection commitee, the NCAA wanted either Wooden or North Carolina's Dean Smith to receive the honor. The AAU's first choice was Adolph Rupp, the legendary coach at the University of Kentucky. But Rupp's health was poor, and the AAU was not about to let the NCAA choose the coach by simply tapping either Wooden or Smith. In fact, Wall says, the committee's eventual vote on Wooden turned out to be a rout, with 38 of the 49 voting against him. As a compromise choice, the selection committee named Iba.

Although Hank Iba was not a bad choice, all in all several individuals resented the heavy-handed way in which the candidacy of Wooden, one of the icons of American basketball, had unceremoniously been dumped. "You have to understand the mentality of the AAU," Wall explained. "They were not basketball people; they were money people. They were there simply because of the fact that they had the money and that's what drove everybody nuts. They had no clue what they were doing in making decisions. They had no athletes, no players, no facilities, no nothing but money. They just were not going to give up control of the Olympic team."

Looking back now, that decision was probably inevitable, concludes Tom Henderson, who was a guard on the team. Henderson also believes that Iba's style of deliberate play, calling for everyone to share the ball on offense, was bound to haunt the U.S. team. Of the decision to go with Iba, he insisted that Wooden was "the best qualified" candidate. "But in the Olympics, they don't change what they do," Henderson says. "They kind of keep with the same thing." However, he added that given the athleticism of the U.S. team, they should have played an up-tempo style against the Soviets in the gold medal game: "We had young deers. Looking back, we should have run them back to Russia."

By June 1971, Iba was, controversially, firmly in place. In the months before the Munich Olympics, an interviewer asked Iba for his greatest thrill. Iba answered, "winning an Olympic gold medal for the United States." It remained to be seen if he could help the country win another one.

And Wooden? He never did coach an Olympic team. In his last book, *The Wisdom of Wooden, My Century On and Off the Court,* Wooden never even mentioned the Olympics. Eventually, UCLA's frigidness toward the Olympics began to fade after Wooden won his 10th and final national championship in 1975, his final year of coaching. In fact, a 1996 attempt to petition the International Olympic Committee to award the 1972 U.S. team retroactive gold medals was spearheaded by a college student named Tony Lattman, the manager at the time of—ironically enough—the UCLA basketball team.

Part II

The Making of a Basketball Team

CHAPTER 9
A Coach Is Dealt His Hand

The physical setting could be a church basement, a city high school, a professional arena, or, in the case of the 1972 U.S. Olympic men's basketball trials, the United States Air Force Academy. Whatever the trappings, every coach of every team at every level starts with the same charge: to mold a group of athletes of disparate abilities, temperaments and personalities—some of whom don't know or particularly like one other— into a cohesive team.

Such was the scene on June 12, 1972, when 59 players milled about a basketball court at the Air Force Academy in the thin mountain air just outside Colorado Springs (elevation 7,200 feet). The high altitude helped players get in shape, the dining and athletic facilities were first-rate, and the isolation from nocturnal temptations kept the players out of trouble.

It was the first day of the trials and Hank Iba, the team's 68-year-old coach, prepared to address the group—one of the few times during the two weeks that the motley collection of NCAA, AAU, NAIA and junior college players and coaches would hear directly from the living legend. As he collected his thoughts, Iba surely knew that his third consecutive Olympic squad would be the last team, at any level, that he would ever coach. And he wasn't sure what to make of what he saw in front of him.

Officially, Iba had nothing to do with who had received invitations, which were issued by the USOC. He had tried to use his influence to coax certain players into attending the trials, to little avail. The cream of college basketball—Julius Erving, Bob McAdoo, Jim Chones, George McGinnis and Brian Taylor—had all claimed hardship and gone pro. Bill Walton, UCLA's standout center, was home resting his knees. Paul Westphal of USC was injured and couldn't make the trials. The players who were there—some of them well known, others unheralded and a few virtually anonymous—were, by and large, young and inexperienced with international basketball.

Players and coaches at the Air Force Academy tryouts at Colorado Springs, Colorado. (Courtesy of the U.S. Olympic Committee).

Although he couldn't yet detect what kind of hand he had been dealt, Iba, by virtue of his previous Olympic coaching experience and nearly four decades in the game, could already see the big picture: the coming end of U.S. Olympic basketball exceptionalism. It would be an understatement to say that Iba took it as a personal affront that other basketball-playing countries were catching up to the United States. Even more galling was the evidence of Americans' nonchalance at the prospect. As far as the media and the country's professional and college basketball fans were concerned, the U.S. simply cruised to the gold medal every four years.

Just weeks before, Iba had revealed to *New York Times* columnist Arthur Daley, who had covered every Olympic basketball tournament since the inaugural event in Berlin, an unease about the impending Munich Games. "In our egotism, we think we're always going to win, but the day has to come when we'll face more than we can handle," Iba said. "Every year, those foreign teams keep getting better and better. Every year, they come closer to bridging the gap." In fact, the projected starting five for the Soviet Union in Munich had cumulatively played in *739* international games.

Whatever combination of players Iba would end up with after these trials, their international experience would be negligible: a few Pan Am Games here, a tour of Europe there.

Crying wolf wasn't Iba's style; when he was confident of America's chances, he said so. At the 1968 Olympics in Mexico City, Iba led the U.S. to a seventh consecutive gold medal in basketball, despite Lew Alcindor's decision to stay away and Iba's questionable move to cut the prolific scorer Pete Maravich from the team. As Iba told the *Washington Post*, "Despite losing Alcindor and those other guys, I always said that the '68 team was a strong one. We knew where we stood because Alcindor and the others turned us down immediately. We then got guys who were winners."

But things had changed since 1968. Iba knew how motivated other countries, particularly the Soviet Union, were to beat the Americans at this game America had invented, no matter how small the stakes or how middling the U.S. contingent. For instance, just about two months before the opening of the 1972 Olympic trials, a Soviet national team trounced a visiting AAU team, 100-83.

During the 1971 Pan American Games in Cali, Colombia, Jim Gudger, the head coach of the U.S. team, watched as the Cuban players outhustled the young Americans. Although he was loath to say much in the ensuing days and weeks after the Games because he felt that any observations would be construed as an excuse, Gudger later wrote in an NCAA coaches' publication that "Cuba came at us with a fierce political desire, complimented by some outstanding basketball... [T]he United States is not a politically oriented country. The intense political desire does not exist among most of our athletes. Yes, we like to win, but the love-of-country-first attitude does not prevail."

Furthermore, to some involved in the U.S. Olympic basketball effort, it seemed obvious that in the year or so before Munich, the international basketball world was actively trying to undermine American dominance. One of the jobs of Herb Mols, the manager of the U.S. national team, was to take care of the details, including the uniforms and travel and tournament logistics. At those same Pan Am Games, Mols wasn't given any information by the officials in Cali, Colombia, about how the tournament would be run, which half of the draw the U.S. was in, or what the Americans' accommodations would be like. FIBA officials just kept repeating that Dr. R. William Jones, the head of the organization, would meet with Mols and the coaches when the team arrived. But Jones was nowhere to be found in Cali, and the meeting never occurred.

None of this, of course, was lost on Iba. As he put it to the *Times'* Arthur Daley, there needed to be a concerted effort on the part of college seniors and the coaches and owners of professional teams to ensure that the best young American players would compete in the Olympics. "They must surely realize that the ambition of all foreign countries is to beat the United States in international basketball," Iba said. "The pros should make an all-out effort to give us the top seniors from the colleges during Pan-American and Olympic years. It would delay the players' signing by only a few weeks, and we could go on dominating international basketball. If it doesn't happen, the road will be rocky, and I can't see a future for the United States in international basketball."

When it came time to speak to the assemblage of players that first day of the trials, the still imposing coach came out and told them to go to Munich and "win it for your country, the United States." He also issued a message of admonition. Because if no else would pay heed to the shrinking talent gap between the U.S. and its rivals, maybe his players would. According to Bach, the former Chicago Bulls assistant coach who served as one of Iba's two assistants for the Munich Games, Iba told the players that, from that moment on they were preparing to play the Soviet Union. "He was aging, but he had a gruff voice," Bach says. "He met the full group and said, 'Here is the assignment. We are going to play a national team in the finals for the gold medal. It's no secret that it's Russia.'"

CHAPTER 10
At the Trials: How It Worked

Gudger, with the help of Mols, made a mighty impression on the powers-that-be within the USOC with a well thought-out debriefing of the Pan Am Games. Gudger argued that the USOC needed to change the way it prepared its national teams, and that the new way of doing things should be in place for the Olympic trials. His main point was that each team needed more time to prepare. The U.S. squad at the Pan Am Games had just 18 days' preparation before flying to Cali. "This would probably be sufficient if we still had the experience from the old AAU industrial league and the Armed Force players to bolster our squad, but we don't," Gudger said, adding presciently: "The Olympic team could be as young and inexperienced as this one."

Responding to the recommendations in Gudger's report, the USOC saw to it that the 1972 Olympic team would spend virtually the entire summer preparing for the Games, which were to begin on August 26. The Air Force Academy trials were just the first step in getting the team ready. After the team was selected, the players would spend three weeks training at the Pearl Harbor naval base, followed by 10 days of games back on the mainland against teams of top professionals. The idea of going to Hawaii stemmed partly from the problems Iba had had in finding enough games for his 1968 Olympic squad; in Pearl Harbor he could schedule numerous games with experienced Armed Forces teams. The American squad might not be as battle-tested as the Soviet or Cuban teams, but they would be as ready as any national team could be in just two months of preparation.

Gudger also recommended that the U.S. employ international officials during the team's training camp and pre-Olympics competitions. Although his advice went unheeded, Gudger certainly was on to something, given the uneven quality of FIBA officials and the language barriers the U.S. would encounter in Munich, where the players and coaches would be able to communicate with few of the referees or scoring-table personnel. To this day, USA basketball does not use FIBA officials as a training device to approximate the conditions of international competition.

The planned format for the trials was straightforward enough. Week one would be devoted to various sets of drills designed to get everyone into the flow, determine what each player could do from a raw physical ability standpoint, and allow the coaches to make preliminary evaluations. Week two was reserved for scrimmaging, with every player assigned to one of eight teams; each team would consist of seven or eight players and compete in seven games.

The process of selecting the 12 players who would represent the United States in Munich was secretive and complicated, quite fitting considering that each of the various basketball organizations wanted its own players to make the team. Twenty officials from the USOC would cast ballots. The votes taken during the first four days would be done by secret ballot; those done the final three days were by open balloting. The USOC was also charged with naming six alternates (although 12 alternates ultimately would be named because their talent level was considered so balanced).

And the coaches? There were two distinct sets of coaches, each with very different roles. Iba had two Olympic team assistants, Don Haskins of the University of Texas El Paso and Johnny Bach of Penn State. Along with Iba, Haskins and Bach would evaluate the players mostly from the stands. Haskins had played for Iba at Oklahoma State. He was the one person during the first day of trials whose name all of the players would have known. His fame preceded him, and his story would eventually be told in the 2003 movie *Glory Road*. Incidentally, after that film was released, anyone who knew Haskins at all would remark that the actual man was a much tougher character than the one who appeared on screen. In 1972, however, neither Haskins nor anybody else could predict just how big of a legend the Kentucky game would take on as the years passed. "I certainly did not expect to be some racial pioneer or change the world," Haskins wrote in his autobiography, which the film was based on. He added: "I've said this many times over the last 40 years, but for a long time I thought winning the national championship was the worst thing ever to happen to me. I wished for a long time that we had never won that game with Kentucky because life would have been a heck of a lot easier for me, my school and my players."

Unlike Haskins, Bach had no close personal ties to Iba. Instead, Bach had been involved with the USOC for 16 years, including assisting with Olympic trials in 1964 and 1968. With his two undergraduate degrees, one from Fordham and one from Brown of the Ivy League, Bach was a full-fledged liberal intellectual in Iba's view. "We had a good relationship, but he would call me an Eastern sophisticate," Bach recalled. "He would say, 'Don't use that college language around me.'" Although the role of assistant coach for the Olympic basketball team may seem like a very prestigious position, according to Bach it was hardly sought after by college coaches. "This was a long summer with no pay involved," Bach said.

The day-to-day sessions and scrimmage teams would be run by a group of eight coaches who ranged from future Hall of Famers like Bobby Knight to obscure Division III coaches like Dean Nicholson, to Armed Forces coaches like Reggie Mitten, from the Air Force Academy. Besides Knight, a fishing buddy of Haskins who had just completed his first season coaching at Indiana, the scrimmage team coaches included Joe B. Hall, a Kentucky assistant who was about to take the head coaching job there; and Robert Davis, head coach of Georgetown College in Kentucky. These eight coaches would not be accompanying the team to Hawaii or Munich. Their roles began and ended at the tryouts in Colorado. Of course, the same could be said for 47 of the 59 aspiring Olympians as well.

CHAPTER 11
The Players

As mixed a bag as the players who reported to the Air Force Academy were, the 28 of them who were representing NCAA teams were the most talented, and therefore had the clear inside track. Even though the biggest names from the college game were either already signed as pros or staying home, there were still many excellent players for the USOC and Iba's staff to choose from. Not all of the players listed below would make the team—but each brought something to the trials that made the final roster decisions very difficult.

Doug Collins was a relatively obscure player from Benton, Illinois, who, early in his high school career, never would have been mistaken for a future Olympian. At the start of his junior year Collins stood just 6 feet tall and weighed only 130 pounds. The whip-thin guard didn't look much like a high school starter, let alone a future No. 1 pick in the NBA draft. But he was lucky enough to be teammates at Benton High with Rick Yunkis, a prolific scorer who would go on to become the career scoring leader at Georgia Tech. Collins grew nearly six inches in the summer between his junior and senior years, just in time to attract the attention of college recruiters who came to watch Yunkis play. Collins eventually chose Illinois State.

Despite blossoming into the nation's third-leading scorer after his junior year in college, Collins wasn't on the radar of the USOC. Big Ten powerhouses like Illinois and Indiana were one thing. Even Indiana State had a basketball reputation in these years before Larry Bird. But Illinois State? Collins, through his college coach, Will Robinson, had asked Illinois State to approach the USOC for him. "Being at Illinois State, we were sort of an unknown," Collins said. "I had to beg to get an invitation to the trials." When Robinson called Collins into his office weeks after the season ended to let him know he had received an invitation to the Olympic trials, Collins became single-minded in his focus. He started going to the university gym to run and lift weights three to four hours a day. "I was on cloud nine that I was going to get a chance," Collins recalled. "I knew we were going to be in the altitude in Colorado Springs so I wanted to be in the best condition."

On day one of the trials, Collins wasn't sure how he would do. He knew that his preparation had put him in an excellent position to do his best, but some of his competitors—Marvin Barnes, Kermit Washington, Ed Ratleff, and John Brown—were some of the strongest players in the country. He had read about these players in newspapers—and now here he was competing against them for a spot.

But Collins quickly discovered that in addition to his scoring ability, his quickness and knack for the ball made him one of the best perimeter defensive players. That was crucial, because it was clear from the first week of hard conditioning drills that this version of the U.S. Olympic basketball team would be built on defense. Looking back, Bach recalled one of Iba's and Haskin's favorite drills, called "five-on-two." Iba believed that any two good defensive players should be able to at least temporarily stop the other team's opposing five. Bach and Haskins would ask if any of the players knew the rules of the drill. When no one answered, one of the assistants would say, "There are no rules." Then the fun began, with the two defenders using whatever means necessary to stop their five opponents from putting the ball in the basket.

It's safe to surmise that **Bobby Jones** was probably the only player arriving at camp that June day whose mother held the single-game scoring record in the family. After high school she went to a finishing school called the National Business College, where she once scored 48 points in a game. Jones's father, too, was an excellent player, having led the University of Oklahoma to the finals of the 1949 NCAA championship, where his team lost to Bob Cousy's Holy Cross squad. Jones, at first, shied away from following his parents into athletics. "I was fairly quiet and uncoordinated and didn't like sports," Jones says. "My dad made me go out in the backyard and do certain drills every day. I didn't really enjoy the drills."

But Jones's height (6-foot-9) and legacy of athleticism finally won out over his reluctance. His basketball skills caught up with his height and he became an All-American at South Mecklenburg High School in Charlotte, North Carolina. Recruited nationally, Jones chose the University of North

Carolina, where the Tar Heels were synonymous with basketball excellence.

As for the Olympic trials, Jones didn't even know they were coming up until coach Dean Smith called him into his office about a week before. Smith told him that Jones's teammate, George Karl—one of several future NBA coaches invited as players to the trials—would be heading to Colorado Springs and that Jones had been invited, too.

Ed Ratleff came to the trials from Long Beach State, where he played for the Shark, Jerry Tarkanian, who would go on to fame as the towel-chomping coach at the University of Nevada, Las Vegas. Growing up in a hardscrabble ghetto in Columbus, Ohio, Ratleff had always thought of himself as more of a baseball than a basketball player. He did, however, win a spot on his varsity basketball team as a seventh-grader, even though he had little idea what he was doing on the court. "I was bad," Ratleff said. "When I say I was bad, I was bad." By the time he was a senior in high school, though, Ratleff was excelling in both sports. His basketball and baseball teams both won state titles, and he was heavily recruited in each sport.

Ratleff ended up being drafted by the Pittsburgh Pirates as a pitcher, and in basketball was most heavily courted by Ohio State and Michigan State. But after a recruiting trip to Long Beach filled with palm trees, California sunsets, and the promise that he could play both baseball and basketball, Ratleff turned down the Pirates offer and the overtures he'd received from Midwest universities. He was hooked on southern California.

Like any other college freshman at the time, Ratleff wasn't allowed to join the varsity team at Long Beach State. Some college players in those days chose to go to junior college their freshman years and transfer as sophomores. Many of the UCLA players opted for this route. Not Ratleff. He enrolled at Long Beach State as a freshman and proved himself right away. In a scrimmage in which the freshmen were mixed with the upperclassmen, Ratleff scored 30 points. The Shark quickly realized the freshman team had a player better than anyone on the varsity. One day Tarkanian gathered the varsity and freshmen teams together at midcourt. He then gave a rare talk about following rules. "You guys know me; I'm a player's coach," he said. "If you give me 100 percent on the court, I don't have a lot of rules. But from now on, there are two rules that everyone in this program must follow. When you are on the floor with Ed Ratleff, get him the ball. The second rule is not to forget the first rule." In the three years Ratleff was at Long Beach State, the team never lost a home game and was often ranked among the top ten teams in the country.

Unlike Ratleff, **Mike Bantom** was a late bloomer. Bantom's career also belies today's notion that youth basketball players need to play on school and travel teams, concentrate on just one sport, practice daily, and attend summer showcase camps to become accomplished. Bantom grew up in the projects of North Philadelphia, playing a little hoops with his friends but never serious, organized basketball until his junior year in high school—and even then he made only the JV team. At Roman Catholic High School in central Philadelphia, coach Speedy Morris decided to make the 6-foot-5 Bantom a project, telling Bantom that he'd work hard with him for one year to try to coax some basketball ability out of his obvious raw talent.

Over the summer between his junior and senior years, Bantom took to the game with the same fierce desire he would display a few years later throughout the Olympic trials. He became a new player that summer in high school, playing all day and late into the night. "I went from being a not-very-good JV player," recalled Bantom, "to being a great senior."

Bantom went on to St. Joseph's, right there in Philadelphia. Part of the city's so-called Big Five (which also included Villanova, Temple, Penn and LaSalle), St. Joe's had a historic attachment to basketball. Bantom's coaches had all been mentored by Dr. Jack Ramsay, who would go on to become an NBA championship coach with the Portland Trail Blazers and a member of the Basketball Hall of Fame. As a freshman, Bantom played for future Los Angeles Lakers coach Paul Westhead, and his varsity coaches were Jack McKinney—who would later coach the Lakers and Indiana Pacers—and Jim Lynam, who would one day be coaching across town for the Philadelphia 76ers. "St. Joe's, for a small school, had a tradition of playing high level basketball and having really great coaches," Bantom said.

In the summer of 1972, Bantom was between his junior and senior years. He was still smarting from the summer before, when he hadn't heard a word about the Pan Am Games, even though some of the players he had bested in collegiate games on his way to averaging 21 points per game as a sophomore were playing (and losing) for their country against Cuba. Bantom made sure to be noticed during his senior year.

When he did receive the invitation to the trials, Bantom still thought St. Joseph's small size would hurt his chances. Not expecting to make the team, he decided that competing for three weeks against the best players in the country would, if nothing else, serve as an excellent yardstick by which to measure himself: how far he had come, and how far he had to go to reach the elite level after his very late start in the game. In other words, he went into the trials with nothing to lose. After all, it was better than staying in Philly "trying to scrounge up pick-up games," he recalled in retrospect.

Tom McMillen was the consummate politician long before he became a member of the U.S. House of Representatives in 1986. While still in high school, McMillen had been appointed by Richard Nixon to the President's Council on Physical Fitness and Sports, and one of the reasons McMillen chose to go to the University of Maryland was its proximity to Washington, D.C.

But choosing Maryland wasn't an easy decision for McMillen, who appeared on the cover of *Sports Illustrated* in February 1970 as the nation's top high school senior. No fewer than 75 times a coach from the University of North Carolina—either head coach Dean Smith or one of his assistants—visited McMillen at his home in the north central Pennsylvania town of Mansfield. In fact, McMillen recalled that telling Coach Smith no was the hardest thing he has ever had to do.

The second reason McMillen chose Maryland illustrates how different his ambitions were than those of other schoolboy basketball stars. Maryland coach Lefty Driesell had the notion that he wanted to build a "UCLA of the East," with McMillen as the anchor and a supporting cast led by fellow recruit Len Elmore. Building something new, rather than being another player in a long line of North Carolina stars, appealed to McMillen. The third reason McMillen chose Maryland was that his father was already sick with the illness that would take his life, and McMillen wanted to play within a reasonable driving distance of home, so his father could see him play. As it turned out, James McMillen did get to attend most of his son's home games at Maryland before passing away in late 1973.

At Maryland, McMillen, a pre-med major who hoped to become a Rhodes Scholar, soon became one of the top center/forwards in the country. His shooting touch from 12 to 15 feet set him apart from other centers, such as Walton and Nater, and in his own way he was equally as effective. With Elmore doing the dirty work under the basket, McMillen thrived, and together they led Maryland to the NIT title in 1972. When it came time for the Olympic trials, McMillen left nothing to chance. Even though he was already a heralded center who had just completed a monster sophomore year, he made sure to write Hank Iba, reminding him how much he wanted to play for his country. Based on his sophomore season, many expected him to emerge as the team's starting center.

The tallest player at the tryouts was somewhat of an oddball to his teammates. **Tom Burleson** grew up a farmer near the tiny North Carolina town of Newland in the western part of the state. As a youth, Burleson was more interested in 4-H and the beef cattle grazing on his family's 65-acre farm than he was in basketball. But his height, 7 feet 2 inches, and natural athleticism—which his father was determined to nurture—eventually brought him to the game.

Each morning, Burleson's father would rouse him for an intense workout: a three-mile run followed by jumping jacks, sit-ups, pull-ups, sprints and push-ups. "My father saw my value as an athletic person in about the third grade," Burleson said. They would follow their routine from the time Burleson was in third grade until he graduated from high school.

The hard work paid off, as it so often does. By his sophomore year in high school, Burleson was dominating his peers, scoring and rebounding in double figures. At North Carolina State, where the former farm boy majored in business agriculture, Burleson improved even more, getting named to the all-ACC rookie team. Like his Olympic tryout buddy Tom McMillen, whom Burleson had tried to convince to come to North Carolina State with him, Burleson graced the cover of *Sports Illustrated*—before he'd played a single varsity game.

Burleson's coach at N.C. State, Norm Sloan, once said, "Tommy's just a good ol' country boy at heart." That country boy image set Burleson apart from the other Olympic players, who regarded him as a flake who liked to tell tall tales. "Everyone thought I was a hillbilly," he later recalled. At the tryouts, Burleson told of a freshman at N.C. State who could jump out of the gym and had outrageous shooting and ball-handling skills, a player who could whup anyone at the tryouts. "Everyone said I was crazy, I was nuts, off the wall," Burleson says. It turns out Burleson was talking about David Thompson, a future NBA star who, though often viewed as an underachiever, may very well have been the best player at the 1972 Olympic trials had he been invited. When it came to Thompson, Burleson would get the last laugh. The two of them teamed up to carry the Wolfpack to the NCAA championship in 1974. In a semifinal showdown against UCLA, Burleson held his own against Walton, helping to end the Bruins' streak of seven straight NCAA championships. Weeks earlier, Burleson played the game of his life, scoring 38 points and gathering 13 rebounds in an overtime win over Maryland in the final of the ACC tournament. Maryland coach Lefty Driesell later called it the greatest performance by a big man that he'd ever seen.

Playing for his country in the Olympics was a goal **Kevin Joyce** harbored even as a child. He had grown up on Long Island in a family of brothers who gravitated toward playing golf at a local course in Bayside, Queens. But Joyce was enamored of stories about famous Olympians like Jim Thorpe. In the fifth-grade, assigned to write his teacher a letter saying what he wanted to be when he grew up, Joyce said he wanted to reach the Olympics in either basketball or baseball. Unbeknown to him, when Joyce was invited to the tryouts years later, his former teacher had the letter ready to show Joyce if he made the cut.

Joyce, a great leaper in his youth, ended up at Archbishop Molloy, one of the top Catholic schools in New York City. It also was a sports powerhouse, thanks in part to Jack Curran, who was during Joyce's time in the midst of a decades-long run as the head basketball and baseball coach. In his senior year, Joyce led both teams to the city championship. In the basketball title game, Molloy beat Power Memorial, Lew Alcindor's alma mater, whose team included the high school All-American and future NBA star Len Elmore. Through Curran, Joyce ended up playing in college for coach Frank McGuire at South Carolina. Perhaps because he was doing what he always planned to do, Joyce entered the tryouts confident he would make the team, unlike a lot of the other participants, who expected to encounter much better players than they were used to.

At the beginning of sixth grade, **Jim Brewer** was 5-foot-5. At the end of eighth grade, he was still only 5-7. That summer, he was growing quite a bit. Finally, at one point during his freshman year, he was measured again—

this time at 6-6. Brewer was moved up the varsity team at Proviso East in Melrose Park, Illinois, the following year. By the time he landed at the University of Minnesota as a high school All-American, he stood 6 feet 9 inches tall.

Brewer, coming from a Big 10 school, wasn't as surprised as some of the other players when his college coach waved Brewer's invitation letter in front of him. Brewer's coach at the tryouts, Joe B. Hall, quickly took Brewer under his wing and made it his business to get Brewer on the team.

When **Jim Forbes** got his letter inviting him to the 1972 Olympic trials, he was going to school at the University of Texas at El Paso, home to one of the signature basketball events of the 20th century. In the 1965-66 season, UTEP, then called Texas Western, fielded a team of all-black starters that beat the all-white lineup of Adolph Rupp's Kentucky Wildcats. Forbes's coach, Don Haskins, had led the Texas Western team in 1966, and was one of Hank Iba's assistants with the Olympic team.

Forbes was a guard locked in a big man's body for as long as he could remember. In high school, even at 6-6, he was put on the wing and asked to handle the ball and shoot from deep because of his skills. "I was really blessed to have a coach that just didn't stick us underneath the basket," Forbes says. But as good as Forbes' high school team was, it could never best a rival team from Wheatley, Texas, led by Dwight Jones, another player invited to the trials. "We didn't win the state title," Forbes explains. "Dwight Jones's team won it three consecutive years."

Dwight Jones was one of the greatest high school players in Texas history, averaging 28 points a game during a career in which Wheatley High won 162 of 164 games. But his college career at the University of Houston had been a different story. Although Houston went 20-7 during the 1971-72 season, the team lost in the first round of the NCAA tournament. It wasn't what was expected from a school that had gone 175-4 in the previous four seasons, and the perception that Jones had an off-season motivated him to show up for the trials with something to prove. From the very first day of the trials, the 6-11 Jones, younger than most of the other players at the camp, impressed Hank Iba and the other coaches with his eye-opening leaping ability.

If it was international experience the U.S. was hurting for at the 1972

Olympic trials, then **Kenny Davis** was the answer. When he arrived at the Air Force Academy, Davis was already a veteran of the World University Games and the Pan American Games. One of the few players at the trials who was married, he was different in yet another way: he was an AAU player, having played for Marathon Oil in the AAU's industrial league.

For Davis, the joy of basketball had always been tempered by the annoyance of being underrated. Even as a high school senior averaging 32 points a game—the highest average in the state—for Wayne County High in Monticello, Kentucky, Davis still didn't make Kentucky's East-West All-Star team or the Kentucky-Indiana All-Star squad. Like Collins and Burleson, the 6-1 guard was another invitee who refused to lose out on an Olympic spot because of the thin Colorado air. "I was in the best shape I have ever been in my life," says Davis, who told himself that if he didn't make the team because he was out of shape, "I would regret it for the rest of my life."

Davis graduated from Georgetown College in Kentucky in 1971 and played AAU ball because, after going to the Pan American Games, he wanted another shot to play for his country. The status of the AAU players was different at the tryouts. While Iba and the Olympic Committee valued their experience and maturity, the word was out among the NCAA players that there was one "slot" reserved for an AAU player. But the truth was that Davis was in better shape than many of the players and he knew the rules of international basketball. As luck would have it, Davis also had the advantage that his college coach, Robert Davis, was asked to be one of the scrimmage coaches at the tryouts, and he got to play for him there.

Tom Henderson upon arriving at the Air Force Academy, was motivated by the fact that if he won a spot on the team, his mother could finally see him play. Henderson was born in South Carolina and moved to New York City in grade school. His father died at age 35 when Henderson, one of eight brothers and sisters, was 12 years old. Henderson's mother didn't have the luxury of attending basketball games at Dewitt Clinton High, where Henderson averaged 20 points as a senior and dominated several All-Star games. "She was a single parent trying to make sure we had food on the table," he recalled. "So she didn't have time."

UCLA's **Swen Nater** was best known in 1972 as Bill Walton's understudy, so very few people knew how good Nater actually was. The duo constituted, perhaps, the best center tandem in the country. Walton would often tell reporters that Nater, the benchwarmer, was the finest center he faced every season, and he had to compete with him every day in practice.

Nater's enthusiasm for making the 1972 Olympic team stood in stark contrast to the seeming indifference that Walton and their legendary coach, John Wooden, showed toward the Olympics. In fact, according to Nater, when the Olympic Committee called Wooden to say that Nater had been invited to the Olympic trials, Wooden called his backup center into his office and asked him whether he wanted to attend. Yes, Nater said right away. "Well, let me warn you," Wooden said. "The Olympic people do not like UCLA. I don't know whether it's jealousy or whatever. But don't expect that they are going to like you."

Nater saw the Munich Olympics as his chance to shine, to be a starting center on the international stage after playing just two or three minutes per game behind Walton at UCLA. Wooden famously had just a seven-man rotation, one sub for the guards and one for the big men. Still, despite his lack of playing time in college, Nater was one of the most mentally and physically strongest players who reported to Colorado Springs.

Nater and his sister spent five years in a Netherlands orphanage before their mother, who had already emigrated to the U.S., could manage to have her children join her in Long Beach, California. "It wasn't fun," Nater recalled, "but kids are resilient. They make the best of things." Being so tall and lanky in high school, he tried out for the basketball team in 11th grade but was cut. He was so sluggish on the court that a physical education teacher once remarked that he'd never seen any living thing "work so hard but move so slow."

But Nater stuck with the game and got a break at tiny Cypress Junior College when his chemistry teacher, who doubled as the assistant basketball coach, invited him to try out. Nater struggled, but he kept getting better. He finally grew into his body, becoming an enormously strong and rangy player who could rebound and block shots and also had advanced skills for a big man, because he had been forced to work on them for so long.

Mike D'Antoni was coming off an Academic All-American season at Marshall in the summer of 1972, an honor shared by Walton. D'Antoni also was cerebral when it came to basketball. His father was a high school coach of 30 years, and decades later D'Antoni himself would go on to coach the New York Knicks. Marshall was ranked as high as eighth in the nation during the 1971-72 season, which helped D'Antoni get noticed by the USOC. When he arrived at the Air Force Academy, one of the first things he noticed was the big hill leading up to the dorms, where D'Antoni met his roommate John Brown.

D'Antoni's stay at the trials didn't quite work out the way he had hoped. For any player who relies on court savvy and knowledge of the game, a 59-player "beauty contest" isn't the best way to get noticed. Still, in the first week, D'Antoni held his own, shooting well in the drills and showing off his crisp passing and impressive stamina. "I just remember the first week being physically really, really rough," D'Antoni recalled. By the start of the games during the second week of tryouts, D'Antoni felt out of his element. Then, in the middle of the second week, D'Antoni suffered a cut to his knee. After the long exhausting walk back to the dorms, he lay down for a nap, only to be found by several of the other players in a daze, wandering the halls. The next step for D'Antoni was the trainer's room and a trip home.

D'Antoni recalled Iba's coaching staff sitting in the stands, monitoring the drills but doing very little instructing, while Bobby Knight in particular played a much more active role. Far from the household name he would become, Knight had just finished his first season at Indiana after coaching at Army for six years. Yet there he was, according to D'Antoni, so intense that he was standing up on a table and screaming at his team to knock the hell out of the opposing players whenever they drove the lane. "If somebody went in for a layup and the defender didn't foul," D'Antoni recalled of Knight, "I remember him jumping up and screaming and yelling, 'Are you a pansy?'"

Three years after his father had left for good, **John Brown** was shooting baskets in his front yard in Dixon, Missouri, when a man pulled over in his car. The man asked Brown, who was nine years old at the time, if he would like to play on his basketball team. The boy said yes. The first game Brown played in, his team lost by a score of 50-0. The next game was barely any better: a 48-4 defeat. But Brown stuck with the game, learned from all those lopsided losses and got better and better as a ballplayer. In his senior year at Dixon High, his team went 36-0 and averaged 100 points a game, 32 of those points coming from Brown.

He went on to the University of Missouri, where Brown averaged close to 40 points a game on the freshman team. With Brown excelling on the varsity over the next three years, Mizzou would just miss out on the NCAA tournament twice. Brown twice earned All-American honors, the first player under Coach Norm Stewart to do so. Arriving at the Olympic tryouts, Brown knew only Iba, whose last year of coaching at Oklahoma State coincided with Brown's first at Missouri. Brown, in other words, was one of the only players in camp whom Iba had either coached or coached against.

Brown likely made an impression on Iba that season, and he certainly made one during the early days of the trials. While some of the players in camp were still growing into their bodies as 20- or 21-year-olds, or were tall but naturally thin like McMillen, Brown, along with Nater and Marvin Barnes, possessed a strong physique. "In hindsight, that team was going to be built around beating the Russians," Brown says. "To beat the Russians, you were going to have to get physical. The two most physical guys on that team would have been myself and Swen Nater."

Brown was also a fast starter, so he impressed very quickly. By his own estimation, he was an atypical player in that he didn't need a lot of warm-up time, a lot of working into a system or getting into a groove. His Missouri squad also played at Colorado once a year, so he understood what the altitude would feel like. "I always had a knack for playing great right at the get-go," Brown says. Within a couple of days, Brown felt as if he had a strong shot of making the team.

Marvin Barnes must have felt the same way about his own chances. He was one player who impressed everyone in the early days of the trials and into the first days of scrimmaging. Barnes, from Providence College, outmuscled everyone for rebounds, ending the scrimmage week as the leading rebounder. He was a strong, imposing and physical—some would say dirty—player. At one point, according to Tom Henderson, McMillen was cutting across the lane and Barnes punched him to the floor. Iba and Bach sent Barnes to the locker room and later grilled him as to why he was trying to hurt his teammates during the tryouts. That incident, one of several such stories of Barnes's aggressive play, probably dashed his chances of making the team. "Marvin Barnes was a thug," recalls Kenny Davis. "I really didn't want anything to do with him." According to D'Antoni, Barnes was actually a great teammate, but played to a different beat. "I later played with him in St. Louis and against him in Europe," D'Antoni said. "Marvin's a great guy; he's just nutty as a fruitcake."

If Iba's words about playing for something other than money counted for anything, then **Kermit Washington** had an inside track on an Olympic spot when he arrived at the trials. Washington had just finished his junior year at American University, where he averaged more than 20 points and 20 rebounds a game (and would finish his career as one of only seven players in NCAA history to average 20 per game in both of those categories). In March of 1972, just after his season had ended, Washington received an offer from the New York Nets of a four-year contract at $100,000 per year. But Washington declined, deciding to stay at American because he felt the school had given him a chance even though he wasn't a standout high school player. Returning to American also meant he could try out for the Olympics. Even as collegiate stars like Erving, McAdoo and Chones were jumping to the pros, Washington had stayed, a poster boy for what Iba and the USOC wanted from sought-after collegians.

The University of Virginia's **Barry Parkhill** was coming off a 1971-72 college season in which he had just been named the ACC player and athlete of the year for averaging 21.6 points per game and leading the Cavaliers to the postseason for just the second time in school history. More so than McMillen, Jones or Joyce, Parkhill was known as a star within the ACC. Years later, he would be named one of the 50 greatest players in conference history. Parkhill was a collegiate All-American and one of the best shooters in the country.

As heralded as Parkhill was, a soon-to-be member of Memphis State, a junior college player from Amarillo College named **Larry Kenon**, also got invited to the trials. Not much was known about Kenon because of his junior college status, but the next season he would lead Memphis State to the NCAA championship game, where they would lose to UCLA. Kenon would average 20.1 points that season. Incidentally, as an indicator that one never knows which college players will succeed or fail in the pros, Parkhill lasted just three years in the ABA, while Kenon went on to become one of the most consistent scorers in the ABA and NBA throughout the 1970s.

CHAPTER 12
The Competition Heats Up

To be sure, there were numerous connections, even some friendships, among the aspiring Olympians. But the players who descended on the Air Force Academy weren't just vying to be on a U.S. national team for two weeks in Munich. For the rest of their lives they would be Olympians—and if all went as expected, gold medal–winning Olympians at that. They also had a clear financial incentive. Bringing home the gold medal would mean more attention from the pros and more potential endorsement opportunities as well. All of which raised the stakes at the Air Force Academy. As Kevin Joyce would later remember it: "The tryout was war. It was probably one of the toughest things I ever did."

College teammates faced off against each other in the scrimmages: Ed Ratleff and Chuck Terry of Long Beach State; Luke Witte and Allan Hornyak of Ohio State; Bobby Jones and George Karl from North Carolina. There were intra-conference dynamics at work as well, as McMillen, Parkhill, Burleson and Joyce all played in the ACC, and each had his own reasons for thinking he had an excellent shot at making the team. Then there were personal rivalries. When Mike Bantom of St. Joseph's walked into the gym, he recognized Kermit Washington of conference rival American University right away and knew that after butting heads with him for three years in collegiate games, now they would be doing so during the trials. Jim Forbes and Dwight Jones knew each other from their Texas high school wars—could Forbes finally come out on top after years of losing state championships to Jones?

There was also some bad blood underneath the surface at the trials, though nothing came of it during the weeks at the Air Force Academy. A few months earlier, in January 1972, Jim Brewer, from the University of Minnesota, and Witte of Ohio State had been involved in one of the uglier brawls in the history of college basketball. Witte was attacked by two of

Brewer's teammates, and Brewer was drawn into the mayhem. The melee left Witte in intensive care for several days. At the Olympic trials, he wasn't the same player he'd been just six months earlier.

To the players, the trials resembled nothing less than Parris Island boot camp. Rise and shine at 7:30 A.M. to begin the two-a-day practices. Not only were the players forbidden to leave the Academy grounds, they could not even *walk* across many parts of the campus. Under Air Force Academy rules, no civilians were allowed to walk across the quadrangle; there were staff sergeants on duty to stop them if they did. "Some of our players wanted to walk through," Bach says, "and special police came right after them and would have normally arrested them." An 11:30 P.M. curfew made sure mischief remained at a minimum. In addition to enduring the grueling two-a-day practices, the players had to trek a mile from the gym to their dorm, mostly up a steep hill. When they walked back up the hill at night after their second practice of the day, in the high elevation, some players thought they wouldn't make it to the dorm.

The players soon discovered that retirement certainly had not mellowed Hank Iba. Like now-storied hockey coach Herb Brooks, who would coach the U.S. Olympic team to glory against the Soviets eight years hence, Iba believed in old-fashioned work: pushing players to exhaustion, even while insisting they implement his complex, ball-control offense. He often reminded his players that the Soviet team had been together for years and would be the toughest they had played in their young careers.

Not surprisingly, the grumbling started quickly. Some of the players complained that Iba's rules made them feel like the Air Force Academy plebes who suffered during the school year because of their low rank. Reporters covering the trials wrote extensively about the players' grievances: curfews more suitable to a high school team on a Spring Break trip, the administration of personality tests, a single television set for the entire dorm where the team was staying, coaches prowling for players who got up to use the restroom after lights out.

Iba also wasn't about to make the tryouts just about basketball. He had always considered a player's home life, background and off-court behavior as being just as important as his basketball ability. To a man like Iba, all of these things mattered, especially when it came to representing the country in the Olympics. But, taken alone, the admonitions for breaching of dinner table etiquette or breaking curfew seemed petty and dated. As one unnamed player confided to Neil Attner of the *Washington Post*, "I guess it's a privilege to be here, but I don't know if I'd come back again." Ed Ratleff had the guts to tell a reporter midway through the trials, "I'm hating the whole thing." Kermit Washington probably didn't help his chances when he told a reporter from a hometown newspaper about the difficult conditions Iba had instituted at the trials. The article's headline—"Kermit Washington: I Pity the Guys Who Make the Team"—implied that Washington didn't plan on making the team.

But according to Iba—who denied to the press either issuing or looking at the results of the personality tests—this was the same formula he had used so successfully in two previous Olympic gold medal campaigns, as well as his sterling 36-year career at Oklahoma State. "The discipline was no different from the 1964 or 1968 teams," he told the *New York Times*. "I don't think you'd let any athletic team stay up all night."

Although Iba was a convenient target, the USOC knew exactly what it was getting when they hired him in 1970 to once again coach the team. And Iba eventually revealed himself during the trials to be a pragmatist with a sense that enough was enough. At some point he decided that with the fatigue level of the players, related to the altitude, it didn't make sense to have a third week of drills after the scrimmages. The players were told the trials would end after just two weeks. In retrospect, it's tough to imagine how much more the coaches could have learned about the players in a third week devoted to further rounds of drills.

Midway through the second week of scrimmages, some of the basketball writers started referring to Dwight Jones as the tryouts' Spencer Haywood, after the NBA star who had his coming out party at the 1968 Olympic trials. But while Jones was turning in consistent performances in the scrimmages, the reality was that no one player was emerging as the definitive "go-to" guy for the team, a deficiency that would cause problems during the Olympic Games. When Haywood clearly became the star of the 1968 trials, part of the reason was that he always wanted the ball at "crunch time."

That's not to say marked differences between players' abilities weren't becoming apparent. Bantom, for example, had come out on fire, scoring much more than anyone had anticipated. He finished the week averaging 16 points and nine rebounds a game. John Brown, too, was playing very well. He recalls being asked after one practice to go out in front of the gym with Swen Nater and Iba to have their photo taken as part of a promotional campaign for the trials. A day or two later Brown broke one of his fingers during practice. He reported to Iba to discuss the injury, fully expecting to be sent home. Instead, Brown recalled, "he told me I had made the team and just to keep it quiet and play defense and rebound the rest of the week."

Most other players weren't so lucky as to have an idea of their fate. Marvin Barnes, from accounts of some of the players who were there, was dominating play on the inside, along with Swen Nater. Nater averaged 21 points per game for the week and was just the kind of physical seven-footer the U.S.—without Walton available—would need against the Soviets. "Swen was tough," remembered Tom Henderson, who himself was turning into an Iba favorite because of his floor-general personality on the court. "Swen was killing people at the trials." In fact, Henderson respected Nater's combination of strength and shooting touch so much that he wondered after the Games why Walton started over Nater at UCLA. McMillen was also playing well, but found himself in an awkward spot. With Nater's dominant play, Brown's toughness even with a broken finger, and Burleson's imposing height and athleticism, McMillen was struggling to find a niche, even though he was consistently hitting his shots around the hoop and averaging 15 points per game.

While the lack of a dominant player at the frontcourt was expected, no one in the backcourt emerged as head-and-shoulders above the competition, either. Collins, the sharpshooting guard from Southern Illinois, scored 30 points in one scrimmage and impressed everyone from the beginning. Henderson was emerging as a good candidate for starting point guard. Joyce and Parkhill were consistently knocking down shots. As for the non-collegians, the AAU players Mike Casey and Bill Newton were holding their own against some of the nation's top college players, but Kenny Davis, with his international experience, was clearly the class of the group. Most players not affiliated with an NCAA program quickly looked overwhelmed by the altitude and overmatched by the energy of the mostly younger collegians.

Adding to the sense of parity, the scrimmage teams were evenly balanced. Six of the teams would finish with identical 4-3 records. But as the scrimmaging heated up during the second week, there was already concern about the style of play that Iba sought. "His court strategy contradicts the playground-style atmosphere of international basketball," wrote Attner of the *Washington Post*.

Iba's style was to remain fairly aloof and let the scrimmage coaches run the teams while he watched from high up in the stands. The players knew Iba was in charge, along with Bach and Haskins, but the trio didn't do much to show it. Bantom doesn't really remember the three principal coaches watching much, but does remember Joe B. Hall and Bobby Knight constantly coaching, letting players have it from the sidelines. Iba himself was often in war story mode, telling tales to reporters, assistants, and various other hangers-on. To some, Iba looked older than his 68 years. Bantom would later tell a reporter: "Iba looked older than that. I was surprised that he could walk most days. He looked like he was about to fall over." The coaches, though, were far more engaged than many of the players realized, even though it was the USOC that would choose most of the players. According to Knight, the scrimmage coaches met frequently with Iba and his assistants. "If you brought up a player, I might say, 'I don't think he can play,'" Knight said. "Or I bring up a player and you might say, 'Yeah, this kid's really good.' I don't know if we met every night, but we met a lot."

Knight was the biggest personality at the tryouts. As D'Antoni and Bantom would be able to recall nearly 40 years later, Knight hollered from the sidelines and stands, not only at the players on his team but also at the referees. At one scrimmage, an official called a technical on Knight (perhaps a first in Olympic trial history). Knight had felt the officials were calling too close of a game, and therefore denying the coaches and USOC officials a chance to evaluate them in the flow of the game. "Goddamn it, let these kids play," Knight shouted. "We want to see who the hell can play." The next day, Knight showed up in a striped referee's shirt and a whistle. But the humor wasn't much appreciated by Iba. The following morning in the cafeteria, Knight walked by Iba and heard him say in a low, stern voice, without looking up from his bowl of cereal: "I don't want to see that goddamn referee shirt again."

As the competition heated up, each scrimmage coach assigned to a team understandably tried to put his players in a position to make the team. But it's easy to see how the process could get distorted. For example, it has been said that Knight told Parkhill before the last game that he had probably already made the team, and that Parkhill should be sure to get the ball to Bobby Jones, so that Jones, already known as a leaper and defensive stalwart, could showcase his limited offensive skills. But Knight's strategy only partially panned out. Parkhill was cut from the team, and it turned out that Jones's outstanding defense and rebounding had likely already earned him one of the coveted spots.

Ed Ratleff's coach was Robert Davis, Kenny Davis's coach from Georgetown College in Kentucky. Three players on that scrimmage team were playing well together and making names for themselves at the trials: Ratleff, Kenny Davis and Forbes. Kermit Washington, a needed big man, came on strong late in the tryouts. As selection day approached, he was "on the bubble." His gaffe of venting to a reporter about the tough conditions notwithstanding, Washington was playing superbly, one of the leading rebounders at the camp.

Given the way Iba approached discipline during the trials, it was inevitable that someone was going to be caught breaking a rule that affected his chances of making the team. According to several of the coaches, on one of the last nights before the team was selected, Barnes and a non-basketball friend were planning on leaving the facility to go out. They inadvertently stumbled across the coaches and USOC officials debating various players' abilities in a conference room, and it was clear that Barnes and his friend were not simply taking a tour of the facility. Although no one ever specifically said that's why Barnes didn't make the team, his transgression likely didn't help.

For Burleson, the tryout came down to a final-day confrontation with Witte, the seven-footer who had been hurt in the brawl with Minnesota during the college season. Witte's coach had a plan to neutralize Burleson by double-teaming him, thereby allowing Witte to shine. The only problem was that Burleson knew Kermit Washington from several basketball camps they had worked together. Washington's double-teams, according to Burleson, were a little late in coming, so Burleson's hook shot wasn't as contested as it might have been. While Washington didn't exactly let Burleson score, he didn't take part in the plan to completely stifle Burleson. As Burleson recalled: "Kermit said, 'I would double-down on you, but this is between you and Luke Witte.'" Witte ended up with nine points and six rebounds; Burleson had a great game with 19 points and 12 rebounds. "Kermit Washington is a part of the reason I was on that team," Burleson said.

Tensions ran high as selection day approached. The members of the USOC had met every night after the previous four days of practice, using a complicated statistical system to rate the players. Still, many spots remained undecided until the final hours. Iba and his coaches took part in the process, but Iba was given only one unchallenged selection. In fact, as in the previous two Olympics, Iba felt as if it wasn't his role to negotiate or plead for certain players. "He said, 'Let the committee pick 11; I want only the choice of the last one,'" Bach recalled. As for hearing of their fate, some of the players remember being called to a breakfast where those who had made the team were announced alphabetically, one by one. Others remember that a list of the players was posted on a bulletin board. It's likely that both were done, but the important fact is that, somehow, these 12 players' names were announced: Bantom, Brewer, Brown, Burleson, Collins, Davis, Henderson, Bobby Jones, Dwight Jones, Joyce, Nater and Ratleff. No Barnes. No Washington. No McMillen. No Parkhill. No Kenon. No Forbes.

A betting man would have put money on a good number of these selections. Brewer, the Big 10 player of the year, could both play center and power forward, as could Bantom. Ratleff, Davis—the only AAU player selected—Joyce and Collins could all score and play good backcourt defense.

Players who made the team but had not been considered shoo-ins a week earlier included Nater, Dwight Jones, Bobby Jones and Brown. Henderson was a long shot before the trials but it came as no shock when Iba selected him as his personal pick, just ahead of Forbes. Burleson marked the biggest surprise, because Nater and McMillen were such well-known stars coming into the trials. Taken together, the team was the youngest and tallest in U.S. Olympic history.

Those who had very strong camps but were snubbed included McMillen, Forbes, Barnes, Washington, Kenon and Parkhill. Interestingly, some of the other players who were cut became famous as coaches, including George Karl, Mike D'Antoni, Bobby Cremins and Greg Popovich, who as of spring 2012 was the longest-tenured coach in the NBA, having led the San Antonio

Spurs to four NBA championships.

The age-old problem for U.S. players trying out for the national team was that America's second and third teams could have played competitively in any international tournament, but only 12 players could go. The embarrassment of riches meant disappointment for these players. In retrospect, Mike Bantom thought that they didn't "pick the best players, but rather the smartest players." Collins, who would go on to coach the Chicago Bulls and the Philadelphia 76ers, put it this way: "I think maybe their thinking was, you had only a short window to try and put this together. So I think they were trying to put together a group that would come together the quickest." Added Ratleff: "I think they picked the 12 guys that were going to stay out of trouble. I think they tried to pick the smartest basketball-wise, because with Hank Iba, the stuff he ran, you had to pick it up quickly."

But the selections at the Air Force Academy did raise some eyebrows, given Iba's style of play. The team that was chosen was young and fast and, aside from Burleson, not particularly big. The question was: With Iba as the coach, would the team play an up-tempo style to match the players' strengths? McMillen, named one of the 12 alternates, soon weighed in. He was stunned that the emergence of Burleson, Bantom and Nater had cost him a spot. "There has to be changes at the top," McMillen said in an interview shortly after being cut. "I don't want it to sound like sour grapes, but there's been talk that the team doesn't have international experience. I have international experience."

With the possible exception of McMillen, Parkhill took the news that he would be an alternate the hardest. Parkhill would later say that, although he would go on to stardom in the ABA, he never fully recovered from not making the team. His sense of failure affected his senior season at the University of Virginia and his subsequent pro career. Knight, after all these years, still doesn't understand why Parkhill didn't make the Olympic team. "Parkhill was about 6-5 and he could shoot and he was a good kid and he was smart," is how Knight described Parkhill. "He absolutely should have made it." As for Kermit Washington, despite his performance on the court, he wasn't even named an alternate, perhaps no coincidence after his outspoken interview.

The full roster of alternates:

- Marvin Barnes, Providence
- Tom McMillen, Maryland
- Mike Casey, AAU player
- Jim Forbes, UTEP
- Mike Green, Louisiana Tech
- Allan Hornyak, Ohio State
- Jim Lister, Sam Houston State
- Bill Newton, AAU player
- Barry Parkhill, Virginia
- Chuck Terry, Long Beach State
- Bob Wilson, Northeastern Junior College
- Luke Witte, Ohio State

Clearly, playing on the previous year's Pan American Games team didn't help much in terms of making the final roster, because three alternates had played on the team. This may have been because that Pan Am team lost, or perhaps it was pure coincidence. In any case, the 12 alternates were told by the Olympic Committee to stay in shape and be ready to report within 12 hours of notification. But none was very hopeful. To make matters worse for McMillen, he learned while en route home that a terrible storm had torn through Pennsylvania and severely damaged his family's home. He would spend the next week working with his brothers to salvage family belongings.

The players who hadn't entered the trials as odd-on favorites only to make the team were thrilled. Nater was looking forward to the Olympics as a world-televised coming-out party, telling reporters: "It's an honor to do something for my country after all it has done for me." Bantom, too, was excited, but also conflicted, remembering that his being an Olympian didn't change things at all for a lot of people he knew. According to Bantom, upon returning to Philadelphia for a few days after the trials, only two people even cared enough to comment about his being named to the team, and that "most of the guys are hanging around, struggling to find a job or hustle a dollar," he said.

Camp broke on June 25, 1972. The players who made the team were given a well-deserved two weeks off until July 10, when they would reconvene to practice at Travis Air Force Base near San Francisco. They would leave for the Naval Submarine Base at Pearl Harbor on July 13. Armed with a legacy handed down from seven previous United States Olympic men's basketball teams, the 12 players left the Air Force Academy charged with defending a 55-0 record and a streak of seven consecutive gold medal victories. All of the players possessed skill, dedication and tenacity. But this team also had weaknesses that would surface during the Olympic Games.

Held Trials Some got

Cut From Team

12 on Team
12 Alternatives

Part III

Blood on the Gym Floor

CHAPTER 13

Blood on the Gym Floor

It was the great American expatriate novelist Henry James who once wrote, "summer afternoon, summer afternoon; to me those have always been the two most beautiful words in the English language." Of course, James never spent a summer afternoon with Hank Iba on a basketball court in Pearl Harbor. Once the 1972 Olympic basketball team had been chosen, it was time to practice—Iba style.

After their grueling tryouts at the Air Force Academy, America's newest basketball Olympians savored what they had achieved. Dwight Jones was able to celebrate almost right away with his mother, who had been staying at a hotel in nearby Colorado Springs to support her son. Tom Henderson spent the days after he made the team back home in New York City. As he was sitting for a haircut in his local barbershop, talk turned to this great young kid from the neighborhood who had just made the Olympic team—a guy named Tom Henderson. Henderson introduced himself, surprising the barber and everyone else in the shop. For John Brown, making the team was one of the most significant days of his life. Four decades later, he still hadn't forgotten the pride he felt.

And the players who had been cut? Most of them either went home or back to campus to collect themselves. Tom McMillen had hoped to be able to tell his ill father, James, and his college coach, Lefty Driesell, that they should book their tickets to Munich. Instead, McMillen went home to help clean up the family home in Pennsylvania after a devastating flood. Jim Forbes was taken aside by Don Haskins, his coach at UTEP, and told to keep sharp in case he was called up to the team. Forbes was a rare breed; he would do as his coach asked, even though he wasn't part of the team anymore. "I was taught that the coach is the one who is in charge," Forbes said. "He's the one who is going to make those final decisions. Whether you agree or disagree with those decisions, you have to go with that." Forbes went home and ran laps in obscurity at his high school track, biding his time.

On July 10, 1972, the players who had made the team regrouped for three days of practice at Travis Air Force Base in San Francisco. Then they left for Hawaii, where they would endure 21 days of training camp at Pearl Harbor. For Iba, Haskins and Johnny Bach, Pearl Harbor was the perfect place to train. First, the military symbolism was obvious at a time when other basketball-playing countries strived to beat the U.S. at its own game. Second, Iba and his assistant coaches could schedule games against a number of armed services teams at the naval submarine base, neighboring Schofield Air Force Barracks and other military installations in and around Pearl Harbor. Finally, the team could be forged in splendid isolation, away from families, girlfriends, hangers-on and the mainland media (at least those who didn't make the trip). In Iba's mind, a pampered group of college boys would be turned into a basketball team that could beat the Soviets.

Holding training camp at Pearl Harbor meant the most to Bach. The son of a merchant marine, Bach had served in the Pacific theater during World War II and lost a brother, who was a bomber pilot, in the war. 'As an old Navy guy, I was happy as hell" to be at Pearl Harbor, Bach said. Also happy to be in Hawaii with the U.S. Olympic contingent was Haskins' wife, Mary. Haskins had decided that he could afford one trip for Mary: Hawaii or Munich. It came as no surprise to him when she chose Hawaii. A friend accompanied her because Haskins, of course, would be otherwise occupied. Incidentally, having his wife there didn't change Haskins' tough outer shell.

After Pearl Harbor, the plan was to return to California on August 4, let the players go home and relax for a few days, and then reconvene August 10 to kick off a five-game series against some rookie all-stars, including Julius Erving, as well as a selection of seasoned pros who had played on the 1960, 1964 and 1968 Olympic teams, among them Oscar Robertson, Terry Dischinger, Bill Bradley, Walt Hazzard and Jerry West. After that, it was on to Munich.

CHAPTER 14

On the Beach

"Hawaii" and "hardship" are two words that don't seem to belong in the same sentence. But for the players, their stay in Hawaii *was* a sentence of sorts—21 days of hard basketball labor. Upon arriving, though, most of the 12 players on the team were just happy to be there. They knew they weren't going to Hawaii to spend time on the beach; most figured correctly that they would barely see the transcendent Oahu coastline throughout their entire stay. They had survived the crucible of the Olympic basketball trials while some notable talents—Marvin Barnes, Kermit Washington, Larry Kenon, Barry Parkhill and Tom McMillen, to name a few—were left by the wayside. And although no one had emerged from the tryouts as the team's undisputed leader, as Spencer Haywood had four years earlier during the trials for the squad that won the gold medal in Mexico City, the team seemed to possess, on paper at least, a good mix of talent and intangibles. Swen Nater had proven a more than capable proxy for Bill Walton, and the roster was filled with pleasant surprises, most notably Henderson, Burleson and Bantom.

But the Hawaiian honeymoon soon ended even for the most ardent Olympian. "It wasn't the finest of conditions," said Doug Collins, looking back. "We went to Pearl Harbor and stayed in barracks and trained, and the 1992 Dream Team went to Monte Carlo and stayed in $1,000-a-night suites. Make no bones about it; that it was one of the toughest three weeks I've ever spent." Given the militarism evident from the first day of training, some of the players felt as if they had actually enrolled in the Navy. The Air Force Academy trials had certainly come with some annoyances from the players' perspectives, but the physical environment was perfectly comfortable: the dorms were typical college-issue and the basketball facilities top-notch.

Pearl Harbor, by contrast, "was a dump," as Jim Brewer put it. "We were in a barracks that I'm not sure was used as a barracks any more," he said. "It was really a militaristic setting." According to Tom Burleson,

Olympic team photo in Pearl Harbor, Hawaii (Swen Nater, top row, 4th from the right) John Brown, 2nd from the right) were still members of the team. (Courtesy of Johnny Bach).

some of the sailors at the base told the players the basketball team had it worse than the military grunts did in boot camp. The players slept on cots in an officers barracks, but even Bach says today that there was really no difference between the officers and the enlistees barracks; the rats and roaches scurrying along the floor clearly didn't care much about military rank and protocol. What's more, Iba had rules governing everything from how the players were to comport themselves at meals with the military personnel to what kind of music they could listen to. "You all better get rid of that monkey music," Henderson remembered the coach telling them.

Too, Hawaii was much hotter and more humid in the summer than the players had expected it to be. There was no air conditioning, which to the uninitiated doesn't sound like much of a problem given the gentle Hawaiian zephyrs for which the islands are famous. But those breezes idle in the August doldrums, leaving heat and humidity as constant companions. The players waking up in the middle of the night were soaked in sweat. The heat was definitely the worst part for John Brown, especially when combined with three-a-day practices held outdoors. "I mean, it was unbelievable," Brown said. "It's like today sending these kids to Iraq in 150-degree temperatures."

To keep cool, the players tried sleeping just in their shorts, but that only provided a feast for the mosquitoes despite webs of netting and liberal doses of repellent. The conditions appalled most of the players. Some of them spoke out about them; others remained stoic. According to Ratleff, one of the stoics, the complaining started right away. "Guys were getting mad," he said. "'We're in Hawaii, we should go to the beach, right? But no; we're at basketball camp.'"

Somewhere, Bill Walton must have been smiling as he read news reports of the team's Spartan conditions. His experience in the World University Games in 1970, and the strict military code the team lived by, was one factor in his decision not to participate in subsequent international competitions. In some ways, it's a tragedy Walton wasn't in Hawaii with the 1972 Olympic team. His reactions to the ascetic physical conditions and to Iba's repressive basketball regime might have entered hoops lore. It would have been interesting to hear what Walton, who made his anti–Vietnam War stance clear many times during his college years, would have had to say about the military overtones of the camp.

The players didn't exactly find relief from their harsh living conditions on the basketball court. The Pearl Harbor workouts would be the toughest that any of the players had ever experienced, no matter their background or basketball pedigree, whether they came from UCLA or UNC, or had burnished their games as youths on urban playgrounds or in rural gyms. Any basketball player knows it's more fun to play games than it is to practice, but with the Olympic squad already chosen there was no need for scrimmaging certain players while others caught their breath. The coaches weren't up in the stands looking at a broad canvas of 50 or 60 men, as they had been at the tryouts. The 12 players in Pearl Harbor, nine of them age 21 or under, *were* the team. There was nothing that stood between them and Iba, their crusty dictator. As Kenny Davis put it: "It was just one team there, and we were under Coach Iba's microscope the whole time." Added Ratleff: "At the Air Force Academy, you practiced and then you played games. You were coming in and out of games. It's easier to play than practice because practice gets monotonous."

Even though the camp was scheduled to last three weeks, many of the players, not surprisingly, remember it as being much longer. Guard Tom Henderson, Iba's personal pick, who would go on to play at the University of

Hawaii after the Olympics, recalls the camp as lasting for at least a month, if not six weeks. It surely seemed longer given the rigorous daily schedule. The players, high-profile athletes but still guests at the base, had to eat at the same time as the pilots and sailors. After a 6:30 wake-up call and a quick breakfast, the team took the court by 7 a.m. They practiced for a few hours and then ate an early lunch before a short rest and the afternoon practice. Next came an early dinner at 5:30 p.m. and, most nights, still another practice.

Jim Brewer, Bobby Jones, Tom Burleson, Doug Collins and Kenny Davis. (Courtesy of Herbert J. Mols family).

CHAPTER 15
Becoming a Team

The team used the same practice court every day: an open-air gym sunk several steps into the ground and protected from the sun and heat by a mere canopy. As the players soon found out, though, the court was sacred ground. On December 7, 1941, more than 400 bodies were laid out on the gym floor as a makeshift morgue in the aftermath of the Japanese attack on Pearl Harbor. A day before the attack, the brass band of the U.S.S. *Arizona* played at the dedication of the new gym. Many of the same soldiers who attended the ceremony would die the next day. "There was blood on the floors that they had varnished over, as a memorial to the sailors," Collins said. The sense of battle, duty and discipline that Iba wanted for the team was embodied in the blood-stained gym floor.

According to Bach, Nater protested that he never had to practice so much at UCLA. But to Iba, the whole idea was to toughen the players up, in as short a time as possible, to beat the Soviets. Not only did the players have to get accustomed to each other, they also needed to learn the international rules and Iba's ball-possession offense. Even though the USOC had factored in more time to get the team ready than in other Olympic years, Iba knew that compared with the virtually professional Soviet Union team, he had little time to bring his players together as a unit. "To practice three times a day, I don't think any one of us liked it," Ratleff said. "But you only have so long to get ready for the Olympics."

From the outset, the conditions on and off the court greatly affected Nater, a son of the progressive UCLA system. UCLA Coach John Wooden was a forerunner to the NBA's Phil Jackson, a coach who personally chose books for his players during his teams' playoff runs. Wooden was famous for mentoring his players rather than berating them when they missed a switch on defense or failed to wait for a screen in the post. Accordingly, Nater was unprepared for coaches' raising their voices, playing mind games or trying to embarrass him. Nater didn't mind Iba so much—Iba had some traits in common with Wooden that Nater respected, such as a strong belief in the team game. It was Haskins and Bach who got under Nater's skin. The kinds of comments that aren't that uncommon in basketball practices from high school onwards—"Get your butt over there on defense!" or "C'mon, rebound!"—Nater took as personal insults and attempts to destroy his spirit.

Nater stood on firmer ground with his teammates, though, in terms of the kind of basketball they were being required to play. "We were talking amongst each other: 'What the hell is this?'" he recalled. "There was no freedom. There was no ability to create a play." And no built-in "breathers," which is what probably upset the players most. As career coaches, Iba, Haskins and Bach knew that players expect a certain number of half-speed days sprinkled in among traditional tough practices over the course of a collegiate season: film sessions, walk-throughs of offensive sets, intrasquad games that conveniently allow subbing in and out so players can rest a bit. At Pearl Harbor, however, the coaches used few of these player-friendly devices. There was just no time. It was hard practice after hard, exhausting practice, followed by more of the same. Most of the players chalked the grueling schedule up to Iba's sadistically wanting to toughen the team up. Said Brewer: "It's just like my dad. He probably figured that we hadn't had it hard enough." If part of Iba's master plan was to provide his players with a common foe in order to foster cohesion, it worked. Various groups of players quickly became tight, walking to practice together, eating at the same tables and sharing inside jokes about the coaches. "There was really nothing to do," Dwight Jones said. "So everywhere we went was together."

Some of the players discovered they could thrive in the demanding environment. John Brown, for example, was playing well even while suffering in the heat and humidity. While some of his teammates bellyached, Brown took to heart Iba's constant reminders that playing for one's country was different from any other kind of basketball. "What Coach Iba instilled in me was patriotic pride," Brown said. Long-time Iba friend and confidante Bobby Knight tells a story that communicates how seriously Iba took his charge of inculcating a sense of national duty in his Olympic teams. When Knight was named coach of the 1984 Olympic team, Iba called him and said: "Now, son, you have to understand that you don't represent your school.

And you don't represent your state. You represent your country." Knight never forgot that admonition. "To me," he said, "that was sacred."

In the heat of those practices, the team's style was forged. Here the players became a team, but not without conflict, exhaustion and hardship. Things started to get more physical as one day melted into the next, as three or four practices turned into eight or nine. The players started to know each other's strengths and weaknesses, as well as the peccadilloes that detracted from their respective games.

Much like teams locked in a seven-game playoff series, nobody had any secrets after a few days. Word got out among the toughest players—guys like Bantom, Brewer and Brown—that the big and strong Nater didn't like it so much when things got chippy. Nater had been so physical at the Olympic trials that players constantly complained about the way he threw his elbows around. On-court tensions with Nater grew worse at Pearl Harbor with the close quarters and incessant practicing. "It started getting real physical in practice, and he became a target," Bantom said. "Every day, Swen was elbowing somebody and he was hitting somebody and he was hitting them the wrong way. At first people complained about it and then it was, like, okay we're going to get you back. So every time we'd scrimmage, people were hitting him and he felt like he was getting the crap beat out of him every day." Iba and the coaches, though, didn't mind the daily battles around the basket, figuring that Soviet big men such as Aleksandr Belov and Ivan Edeshko would be at least as tough as Nater and Brown. "No one saw the beach or took a swim," Bach told Carson Cunningham in *American Hoops: U.S. Men's Olympic Basketball from Berlin to Beijing*. "It was almost warlike the way they worked."

At one point, Iba's voice started to give out under the strain of orchestrating practice after practice. It didn't help that the court was open-air, with no walls for his words to bounce off. Soon Haskins was running the practices, his piercing yells—Haskins, a hunter, was known to have an uncanny coyote call—bellowing across the court. Despite being a paragon of basketball liberalism for what he achieved with his Texas Tech team against Kentucky years earlier, Haskins, in the words of Bantom, was "this big, redneck-looking guy." What Haskins was personally like can be gleaned from an incident that would occur before the third exhibition game against the pros in Los Angeles, a couple of weeks after training camp. Bach and Haskins were lost in South-Central L.A. Spying a group of six seemingly thuggish men on the corner, Haskins decided that he would ask them for directions to the Forum, the arena where the Lakers played at the time and where the exhibition was to be held. Bach cringed in his seat, as Haskins pulled up, rolled down his window, and yelled, "Girls, can you tell me where the stadium is?" In terms of personal style, Bach was more the quiet, tactical type looking for chances to influence Iba's decisions on defense, though he couldn't convince Iba to put much time into practicing the 2-3 zone for which Bach was best known.

CHAPTER 16
Plan A

At Pearl Harbor Iba emphasized tough man-to-man defense and ball control, an offensive style the players abhorred. But to Iba, who knew more about the international game than anyone, the best way to beat the talented, experienced Soviets in two month's time was to build a team based on waves of players, all in great shape, playing a ball-control offense that would eventually tire the Soviets, who had a great starting five but little depth. In general, Iba had always felt the international teams, including the Soviet Union, were not as developed defensively as offensively, and in Munich he planned on exploiting that weakness. If a team could pass the ball several times and avoid one-on-one basketball, the Soviet defense just might break down.

For this theory to work, nurturing a few star scorers wasn't going to cut it. The players had to transform themselves into interchangeable pawns in a larger chess game. Creating such a dynamic was the point of everything going at the training camp: the military overtones; the 12 cots in one room; the strict rules; and the policy of no exceptions to rules that sounded arbitrary, such as no food in the barracks. The overriding goal was simple: break the players down as individuals and form one coordinated unit, with a sole focus on beating the Soviets. To emphasize the point, the coaches, mid-practice, would often warn the players about the other teams at the Olympics, the Soviets in particular. According to Bantom, the coaches tried to "scare" the players with tales of how the Russians were going to manhandle them.

Other evidence points to Iba's fixation that summer with how to solve the Soviets. Steve Haskins, Don Haskins' son, was 14 years old in August 1972. Though Steve didn't join his parents on the trip to Hawaii, his father told him several times that summer that, despite America's Olympic unbeaten streak and all that came with it, the coaches considered the U.S. the clear underdog going into the Munich Games. Haskins told his son that

Iba felt that if his team could "shorten the game" by working for a good shot on every offensive possession, they would win. That's why, about midway through the grueling camp, Iba scrawled the number "50" on a blackboard in the locker room. Iba then dramatically turned to the team and said, "If we keep Russia under 50 points, we'll beat them." Iba's incessant drilling of his players on how to run their offense, his insistence on five or six passes each time down court, was designed to control the tempo of the game and keep it low-scoring.

Haskins also told his son that Iba believed if the Russians became exhausted, they would end up choking in a tight game—that they weren't mentally ready to break the United States' stronghold on Olympic basketball gold. So that was Plan A: grind the Russians down and count on pulling out a close game at the end. But Plan A was never made explicit, or even implicit, to the American players, who were kept in the dark about virtually everything except for when their next practice was. One reason for their ignorance might have been the extreme of Plan B.

CHAPTER 17
Plan B

That Bill Walton refused to attend the trials partly to avoid just such a training camp as what the Olympic team experienced at Pearl Harbor didn't mean the USOC had given up on the big redhead. Even as the three-a-day practices began in earnest, negotiations were ongoing with Ernie Vandeweghe, Walton's adviser, to create a scenario in which Walton could still play. According to Knight and several members of the team, it was understood that Walton would be welcome to fly to Munich for the opening ceremonies at the last minute. At one point Vandeweghe called to tell Bach, the point person for this project, that Walton still might play. Bach took this information to Iba, but the old coach's response said it all: "He refused to go to the trials. Why should we select a player now?"

But at least a couple of the players say today that they would have been fine with Walton's joining them, as it almost assuredly would have meant a gold medal. Ratleff, for one, said he would have had no problem if Walton had waltzed onto the plane, ready to play, just as the team was leaving for Munich. No Air Force Academy, no Pearl Harbor, no five physical games against the pros. Asked what he would have said to Walton at that point, Ratleff replied, "Welcome aboard."

But Ratleff also said that because of racial tensions that were very much in the air at the time, some of his fellow black players might have raised objections. "You still had the white-and-black thing going," Ratleff said. "Whereas the white guys might think, that's okay, black guys might not have." But skin color has nothing to do with it as far as Kenny Davis is concerned. When asked about Knight's comment that Walton had a free pass to just show up and play in the Olympics, Davis, the guard who had the most international experience of any of the players, says that such an occurrence would have been deeply problematic for the players who had gone through every step mandated by the USOC "The rest of us would have resented that, with what we had to go through to get to that point," Davis said. "Especially going through Pearl Harbor."

Brown, too, says that seeing Walton step on a plane to go to Munich would have been "a tough sell with the rest of the guys." As it would eventually turn out, however, two members of the team in Munich *didn't* have to go through the entire Pearl Harbor camp, and one player on the final squad never stepped foot in Hawaii that summer. But Iba nixed the idea of taking Walton when Bach brought him Vandeweghe's message. That was the end of the Walton kabuki dance for a while, at least until events later in training camp again raised the possibility of his riding to the rescue.

CHAPTER 18
A Player Departs

Meanwhile, Walton's UCLA sidekick Nater continued to have a hard time continuing what he started in Colorado. One of the reasons Nater had impressed so much at the Olympic trials was the perception of him as a career backup; not much was really expected of him. Nater himself pretty much surmised that, showing up as a second-string center, he wasn't going to get the ball much at the trials. To prepare, he practiced in the driveway of his future mother-in-law's house wearing a 30-pound weight jacket. "I just shot and shot and shot, and that's basically how I practiced," Nater said. The unusual regimen paid off as he lit up the Air Force Academy with his offensive skills. But during the first few practices in Hawaii, his performance had been notably worse than at the trials, especially as other players returned his physical play in kind. His shooting wasn't as sharp, his rebounding lackadaisical, and the negative vibe he felt from the coaching staff wasn't helping his confidence. But most important, Nater wasn't eating. The team, in keeping with the base's cafeteria schedule, ate when the military personnel ate. Nater simply couldn't force himself to eat so quickly after practice; by his own estimate, he lost 20 to 25 pounds in five days.

"I sweat more than anybody—I just pour out sweat," Nater said. "So the first thing I need to do after practice is to fill up with Gatorade or water. Since that fills you up, I don't feel hungry for the first 45 minutes after practice." After the first day of practice, Nater was already concerned, and asked if he could get some food in his room between practices. "They said, 'We can't treat you differently than anyone else. If you can't eat during those times, then you just can't eat,'" Nater recalled. The commissary did keep separate hours from the main cafeteria, but since he had no money, Nater couldn't avail himself of this option. He couldn't even bring a tray of food from the cafeteria back to his room. Mess sergeants stood by the garbage cans, making sure trays were empty and no one was taking food out of the cafeteria. "The rule in the military is take all you want, but eat everything you take," Bach said. So Nater wasn't leaving the cafeteria with any extra food.

A few days later, Nater tried again with the coaches. "I am going to ask you guys one more time because as you can see, I'm losing weight and I'm weak," he recalled saying. The reply? "We can't help you."

It was at that point that Nater decided to leave the team. He went to a neighboring beach to kill time. That's where Bach found him and gave him a plane ticket home. Although Nater had been telling anyone who would listen that he wasn't eating, the 20 to 25 pounds he lost wasn't particularly noticeable on such a big man. As a result, none of his teammates seemed to realize how mentally and physically close to the edge he was at the time. Then, one day Kevin Joyce just saw him walking down the road out of the compound. Seeking to explain Nater's decision, Bill Summers, the U.S. Olympic basketball chairman, told the press Nater had "checked off the plusses and minuses and decided to go home." Iba said it was the first time someone had made the Olympic team and quit so late in the process.

Even today, 40 years later, his fellow teammates aren't fully sure why Nater left. It was likely that the food issue was just the final straw. The subtext was that Nater—and he was far from the only one—didn't care for the militaristic overtones of the camp. And according to Brewer, Nater also stated that he missed his girlfriend. "He had that faraway look," Brewer said. Ratleff has another theory: "I knew he was a UCLA guy and I know how UCLA guys felt. I heard about UCLA guys who would not go to the Olympics because Wooden was not asked to coach."

On the plane ride home, Nater felt heartsick that he had to leave the team. But there was a silver lining. "I'm thinking I'm glad this is over because now I can finally get a meal on the plane I could eat," Nater said. "It was just crazy." Ironically or not, a few days after he left, the team was moved out of the infested dormitory and into some more tolerable apartments on the grounds of the base.

Nater's take today is that Wooden was right in his warning to Nater when he received his invitation to the tryout. Nater believes the 1972 Olympic coaches didn't want players from UCLA, were forced to take Nater after he excelled at the trials, and were relieved to be rid of him when he quit the team during training camp. When Nater returned to campus and saw Wooden, the Wizard of Westwood gave him a knowing smile, indicating it was his belief all along that Nater's chances to be on the Olympic team would be torpedoed at the submarine base. But why would the Olympic coaches have it in for John Wooden and UCLA? "Coach Wooden was different," Nater said. "He didn't schmooze with all those guys. They never wanted me on the team because I was from UCLA. They had to have me because I scored all those points" at the tryouts.

The U.S. Olympic team was now bereft of the top two centers in the college game, perhaps two of the best centers anywhere. Nater's departure left a gaping hole even bigger than his humongous physical frame. With his experience sparring with Walton for years and his sheer size and strength, Nater was exactly who was needed against the older, more experienced Russians. By dint of his position on the low post, Nater could have been the team's number one option on offense. "Our problem on that team was that we didn't have a go-to guy when the chips were down," Kenny Davis said. "You can't depend on a guard to do that. Dwight Jones, bless his heart, was as good as he could be at that point, but he was small for a center. Tom Burleson was too young and inexperienced and wasn't that good of a player at that time. Swen Nater would have made quite a bit of difference."

Over all, though, the players were mixed in their opinions on Nater's departure. Like Davis, John Brown felt that even though Nater may have not completely lived up to his 7-foot-1 frame, he would have been a key weapon against the Soviets, helping to "absolutely dominate them." Bantom, however, disagreed. Nater could rebound, Bantom said, "but he had no clue how to play the game. He couldn't pass, he couldn't defend. He was just big and strong." According to Bach, when Nater left, the players realized the team had lost a true talent, but nobody cared that much.

If his performance in the NBA is any indication, Nater indeed would have been helpful against the Soviets, at least on the glass. Among other accomplishments, Nater is the only player to lead the league in rebounding without having ever started a single game in college. One can draw a direct line, in fact, between Nater and the ascension of other European big men who would find success in the NBA: Arvydas Sabonis, Rik Smits, Vlade Divac, Pau Gasol and Dirk Nowitzki, who in 2011 led the Dallas Mavericks to the NBA championship.

With Nater gone, the Olympic players were anxious to see who would replace him. Could one UCLA center be replaced by another? But Iba had already come out against the idea of bringing in Walton and, besides, there were 12 very good players in the alternate pool. In fact, Iba and the USOC worked extremely fast. It couldn't have been more than a few hours after Nater officially quit that Tom McMillen got the call. Nater quit on a Tuesday and it was reported in *The New York Times* the next day that McMillen would be replacing him. But McMillen—always reflective and ever the politician—first had to think about it a little bit, and his college coach, Lefty Driesell, was the individual whose opinion he valued most. Driesell told him, in so many words, It's the Olympics; swallow your pride and go. "I got over the disappointment," McMillen said of having been cut from the team after the tryout. "You just went off and did it."

So within a couple of days, in came McMillen to Pearl Harbor, armed with his trademark stack of books. As McMillen did everywhere he went, he spent his spare time at the training camp reading. On the court, however, his natural curiosity was something Iba could do without. The intellectual McMillen, a much different person and player from Nater, soon become a lightning rod for Iba's criticism. At one point, McMillen raised his hand and Iba told him to "save the questions for Lefty Driesell." McMillen's bookishness didn't always play well with his teammates, either, but for the most part they simply considered him eccentric and more or less left him alone. Most of the players remember the future congressman on bus trips or between practices with his nose buried in a book. "He was real bright," Ratleff said. "He used to read all the time."

McMillen was, according to Jim Brewer, "a walking trivia machine." He soon got a chance to show the depth of his knowledge. To break up the monotony of training camp, the coaches arranged a day for the team to experience the history of Pearl Harbor. The team toured, among other places, an enormous airplane hangar where they got a look at a secret Naval "skunkworks," including a group of helicopter prototypes. McMillen started estimating the costs of the helicopters and what portion of the country's budget must have been spent on them, drawing several teammates into a debate about the military budget and the war in Vietnam. The team then moved on to the U.S.S. Arizona memorial. While the Japanese sneak attack that brought the United States into World War II was ancient history to the players, Bach and the other coaches had the perspective of middle age to know that three decades wasn't a long time at all. For them the meaning of Pearl Harbor was still fresh in their minds, for the players not so much.

The truth was that the players were so exhausted they didn't even need diversions. There were on-base activities the players could engage in, but bowling or watching a movie with their coaches probably just emphasized for 21-year-olds their inability to get off the base. One day, Iba told Bach and Haskins that the team had been invited to an evening luau. His instructions to his assistant coaches: "You bring those players back at 11." The implication was that anybody who violated curfew would not be going to Munich. Bach told the team that the Marine Corps sergeant driving the bus would be leaving to make it back exactly at 11 p.m., and he wouldn't be waiting for anyone. No one missed the bus.

At one point, Bach and Davis went on their own misadventure. Bach, a former Navy lieutenant, took Davis on a hair-raising flight over Oahu in a private plane. Bach told Davis of plans to rent a plane and asked if Davis wanted to fly with him. Davis, who tended to do what coaches asked of him, decided that Bach, as a pilot, must know what he was doing, and climbed into the two-seater. "I was 23 years old and I wanted to play," Davis said. Bach wanted to trace the path that the Japanese pilots took in their sneak attack on Pearl Harbor. It was a beautiful sunny day in Honolulu, and the flight seemed to be going fine when Bach nonchalantly pointed out that the fuel gauge showed empty. "I'm sure we've got fuel," he told Davis. "But just to make sure I'm going to turn around and go back." Bach tried calling the tower to ask if they could land immediately with the regular air traffic at the main international airport, but there was no radio signal. Somehow, the plane's electricity had failed. Still, Davis wasn't too concerned, since Bach seemed calm and collected.

But actually Bach was worried. Although protocol dictated that pilots of planes with no communications capacity were to stay away from the landing area in a holding spot, Bach didn't want to stay up their too long because of his uncertainly over the fuel. "The whole idea was, how can I land the plane?" Bach said. "I can't communicate to one of the biggest airports in the goddamn islands." After he saw a big plane, or a "heavy," land, Bach figured air traffic control wouldn't be landing two heavies in a row. He approached the field in a way that the tower could see him, nice and low at 1,200 feet. He didn't hear any other traffic coming in, so he just flew on in and landed. Not knowing where to taxi, Bach had enough sense to stay away from the runway where the big plane had landed a few minutes earlier. Bach followed the signs for "general aviation," and cut the engine. By the time he brought it to a stop, the unlisted plane making an unauthorized landing was surrounded by Air Force personnel. Now that they were on the ground, Davis looked over at Bach and saw that his hands were shaking and the coach was profusely sweating. Bach, attempting to retrace the Japanese path to Pearl Harbor, ended up engaging in his own sneak attack.

Ironically, given all the military imagery that Iba and his coaches had conjured up for the training camp, the Munich Games were coming in a period of relative calm in the cold war between the United States and the Soviet Union. Just weeks before, Nixon had become the first sitting U.S. president to visit the Soviet Union, for the Strategic Arms Limitation Talks in May 1972. The Nixon administration was pushing hard for an election year breakthrough that would improve relations between the two countries and signal to a war-weary U.S. public that Nixon, too, wanted peace with the Communist Bloc.

Contrary to what could have been expected of the shifty-eyed U.S. president and the ostensibly dour Soviet leader Leonid Brezhnev, the two often used humor to diffuse tensions at the various meetings and negotiations in Moscow. For example, when President Nixon hosted a dinner at the U.S. Embassy one night after a long day of grain-price negotiations, the servers had for some reason neglected to put bread on the tables. As Nixon passed along a plate of nuts instead, William Safire of the *New York Times* reported, one of the Soviet officials observed to First Lady Pat Nixon, "No wonder you Americans have so much grain—you don't eat bread." On the same trip, at a crucial point during the SALT negotiations in the Kremlin, Secretary of State Henry Kissinger held up a sheet of paper he had been writing on and asked a "runner" if some copies could be quickly made. Andrei Gromyko, the Soviet minister of foreign affairs, interjected that the assistant needn't bother; hidden cameras in the Kremlin had already no doubt made the copies and they could be produced immediately.

In his acceptance speech for the Republican nomination in late August 1972, just before the Olympics were to start, Nixon touted his accomplishments at achieving détente with the Soviet Union and the People's Republic of China, which Nixon had visited in February, ending 25 years of diplomatic silence between the U.S. and China. "When the history of this period is written," Nixon said, "I believe it will be recorded that our most significant contribution to peace resulted from our trips to Peking and Moscow ... In our relations with the Soviet Union we have moved from confrontation to negotiation and then to cooperation in the interest of peace." Vice President Spiro Agnew asserted that with his talks with the Soviet Union and China, Nixon had "given new heart to people everywhere." Nixon, of course, had no way of knowing that after all he had done to find common ground with the Soviet Union, it would be a basketball game a few days hence that would help reignite tensions between the two superpowers.

Additional intrigue was added to a potential Olympic gold medal game between the U.S. and the Soviet Union thanks to two other high-profile East-West competitions that summer. One was the Hockey Summit pitting the Canadian national team against a team of Soviet all-stars, to be hosted jointly in Canada and the Soviet Union in late September, overlapping with the Olympic Games. Although the Americans were not involved, the series drew close attention in the States, as with anything to do with the big, bad Soviet hockey teams. The second competition was more rarified, an event for the ages: a battle for the world championship in chess. While the basketball team was in Pearl Harbor, the world's attention was glued to the unlikely venue of Reykjavik, Iceland, where a heated, seven-week-long battle of attrition was being fought between American Bobby Fischer and Boris Spassky of the Soviet Union.

Although many Americans today are familiar with Fischer, they might not know how rare it was for anyone to challenge the Soviets (actually, the Russians, as the champions from the Soviet Union were invariably Russian) for the title of world chess champion. One Soviet grandmaster after another had held the distinction for 35 consecutive years, nearly as long as the 40-year Olympic unbeaten streak of the U.S. basketball team. One prominent Soviet chess champion described the importance of chess to the Soviet Union this way, according to sports historian Christopher Clark Elzey, in his *Munich*

1972: Sport, Politics and Tragedy: "The traits of the Soviet man in general—his spirit of invention, his resourcefulness, his dislike of resting on his laurels, his bold solution to theoretical problems, an exacting critical attitude toward himself—exercised their influence on the Soviet school" of chess. Fischer, on the other hand, epitomized individuality. He wasn't exactly a team player in the mode of the Hank Iba fraternity man. A *Time* magazine article on Fischer in July 1972 characterized his behavior by saying he "walked out of tournaments. He complained about the lighting, the scheduling, the spectators, the air conditioning, the living conditions, the purses." Spassky, the reigning world champ, was the polar opposite. He looked precisely as the average American imagined that a cold and calculating—if elegantly attired—Soviet chess champion would.

Fischer, boyish-looking at age 29, was at the peak of his powers and his petulance, foreshadowing the bizarre turn his life would take in the ensuing years when he became a veritable hermit. First, he went to his favorite trick of demanding a bigger purse. A well-to-do English chess fan—is there any other kind of English chess fan?—ponied up $120,000 to increase the prize money.

Despite Fischer's enigmatic behavior, or maybe because of it, the chess championship captured the attention of the American public as never before (or since, for that matter). The two players even sparred like Cold War spies. According to the August 23 *New York Times,* the 17th game of the match was adjourned when Spassky's handlers accused the Americans of using "electronic devices and a chemical substance" to derail him. On September 1, the day the U.S. basketball team trounced Egypt in the first round of the Olympics, Spassky conceded the historic match, making Fischer the first—and, as of 40 years later, still only—American to be crowned world chess champion.

So from Moscow to Peking to Reykjavik, there was plenty going on in the world concerning the two Cold War rivals, but none of it penetrated the black hole of the Pearl Harbor training camp, which remained as shut tight as any Communist gulag. With the Nater drama complete, the players settled into their roles, each establishing his own individuality. Bobby Jones's strategy was the same as always: keep to himself. Jones would return from practice and take a nap, then maybe chat with a teammate for a few minutes en route back to the practice court. "I really didn't have a whole lot of interaction with the guys," Jones said. For his part, Dwight Jones concentrated just on basketball and tried not to get caught up in the complaining about Iba's old-fashioned system, the international rules, or who was going home and who was staying. "I wasn't dissecting who's there, who wasn't there," Jones said. "Just give me the basketball and I'm going to play. That's all I thought about."

McMillen may have spent much of his time studying and reading, but he did warm up to Burleson, who was still perceived by his other teammates as being odd. Burleson also spent time with Kenny Davis and Doug Collins, who was quickly emerging as a vocal leader on the team. The players, by their own admission, tended to socialize along racial lines, although Burleson recalls, "Our whole team bonded in Hawaii."

Kevin Joyce was the joker—he would talk back to Iba, trying to josh around with the old man. "Everything he did was funny," Dwight Jones said of Joyce. With a week left in camp, Joyce, the Queens kid who played his college ball at South Carolina, found out just how interchangeable players on the team were to Iba. Joyce suffered a spasm in his back and missed a practice. He actually wasn't very concerned, as he had experienced these before and knew the drill: they would go away in about four days. Iba, by his standards, made a grand compromise: Joyce had 48 hours to show up and start practicing again, or he would be sent home. There weren't 12 alternates for nothing.

A player much admired by his teammates was Jim Brewer, who may have been the best defender in camp, a Dennis Rodman 25 years ahead of his time. Brewer didn't have much of an offensive game, but he could rebound, block shots and defend. "He was probably the only guy drafted number two in the league who may not have even averaged 10 points a game in college," said Bantom.

Even though Iba had hoped to have eight to ten exhibition games at Pearl Harbor, the team played only four. Their "home" games were played in the isolation of the base, their "away" games at the gym of whichever military outfit they were up against. Because those games were closed to the public, there was no crowd, no cheering, no feeling that the players were getting away from their isolation. Davis, who at nearly 24 was the oldest player on the team, saw himself in some of their exhibition opponents, players a little more mature and experienced. He thought he understood why Iba wanted to play those teams, surmising that the coach "felt like they were similar to what the Russians would be like." Despite the team's sweeping all four games, Iba wasn't satisfied that all the players had internalized the slow-it-down, cautious brand of basketball he felt was needed to beat the Soviets. As the team prepared to leave Hawaii on August 3, Iba told the *New York Times* that the team still had "fellows who take too many chances."

On the last day of the training camp in Hawaii, John Brown went to make a cut toward the basket. Not only did he sprain an ankle on the play, he felt deeper pain in his foot as well, the same foot that had been giving him trouble during the collegiate season. At first, he didn't realize how badly he was hurt. He could move forward fine. But then he tried cutting again, and he couldn't do it. An initial X-ray found no fracture, so Brown and the coaching staff figured he could rest the ankle and then be ready to go.

Notes who made the U.S
Basketball team went home
ne of his unwillingness
to cut while the U.S
played Russia 4 times in the skins

CHAPTER 19
Unleashed

Even with the cloud of uncertainty surrounding Brown's condition, there was no doubt the team was ready to play as they headed home on August 4. After a few days off, the team regrouped in Dayton to start a series of games against the pros. Released from their Hawaiian purgatory into the relative freedom of actual games against opponents with fans in the seats, the team played with cohesion, discipline and hustle. In the first game, on August 10, they went up against a team led by Oscar Robertson and Spencer Haywood as well as the former Olympians Charlie Scott and Bill Bradley. The national team beat the pros, 65-52. The next night in Louisville, Iba's guys won again, also by a 13-point margin.

Although the wins proved the players had become a team, it wasn't all good news. When the exhibition series in the States began, Brown still couldn't do anything on the court, even after the short layoff. With the swelling in his ankle down, Brown looked ready to play but still couldn't cut left or right. Iba and the team trainer suggested Brown start running stadium steps. The extra work didn't help. At one point, Brown was convinced the coaching staff thought he was faking the injury. By the time the team arrived in Los Angeles for the third game, it was clear the foot needed to be looked at again. A second X-ray revealed a stress fracture, which can sometimes take a few days to show up. No one realized it at the time, but Brown had broken his foot on the same play that he had sprained his ankle. The team doctor for the Los Angeles Lakers examined him and said that to properly recover, Brown would need surgery and a bone graft to repair the fracture. After the Olympians eked out a victory by two points, Iba sat down with Brown.

According to Brown, Iba's opinion was that with the likelihood of Brown's being a high draft pick, he should undergo the surgery, or whatever medical course was recommended, right away. Never did Iba suggest Brown should go to Munich as a member of the team. Whether it was for financial reasons, team chemistry, or just that the coaches didn't want a player at the Olympics who wasn't competing, Brown was dropped from the final roster. He was told that when the team flew to Greensboro, North Carolina, for its next exhibition game, he would not be on the plane.

The night the team left for Greensboro, Brown sat alone crying in the Los Angeles airport, waiting for his own flight back home. The one player who had most embraced Iba's Cold War message of winning for national pride was heading back to Missouri an emotional wreck, his Olympic dream derailed. He didn't even get the chance to say goodbye to his teammates. "We felt bad for John because he went through Pearl Harbor with us," Kenny Davis said. But Brown had become a casualty, which made him different from the rest of the players. He was no longer one of the warriors. Even though in his heart he knew Iba was looking out for his best interest, Brown had become, as he put it, "kind of an outcast fairly quickly."

As it turned out, Brown never did have the surgery. His doctors back home recommended only rest, and Brown bounced back to have an excellent senior year at Missouri. Although he later played in the NBA with some of his former Olympic teammates—Henderson, McMillen and Dwight Jones—none of them ever discussed the Munich Games with him, even though he would ask about them. "It's almost like a battle that you don't talk about, where bad things happened," Brown said. "Guys weren't ready to share their experiences." Today, Brown still considers himself a member of the team, and recalls his experience with a mixture of pride and bitterness. After all he had gone through, it just didn't seem right not to be invited to go and cheer the team on. "I was never invited to Munich," he said, "or I would have tried to go." What's more, Brown, who was broke at the time, was looking forward to the Sears clothes that every Olympian was to get at a White House send-off before the Games.

With Brown unable to play, Iba needed to select another alternate. An obvious choice was Forbes, who had played well at the trials but got caught up in the same numbers game McMillen had after the emergence of Bantom and Burleson. Forbes came with one big advantage, though: he more or less knew Iba's system, because Haskins used large portions of it at UTEP. But before the call went out to Forbes, there was one other possibility (of course):

Walton. According to Bach, Walton was still a possibility at that late date. And it would have worked for everyone. After all, someone was going to be named to the team who hadn't gone through the crucible of Pearl Harbor, so why not Walton? Everyone would get what they wanted: Walton could just show up in Washington with the other Olympians for the departure to Munich. Iba would be getting the best young center in the world. The USOC would get its wish to have the U.S. team become the automatic favorite over the Soviets. But it wasn't to be. Forbes got the call that Brown had injured himself and that Forbes was needed in Washington, D.C. When the time came to meet up with his teammates, Forbes was told he hadn't missed anything in Hawaii, just a lot of three-a-day practices and mosquito bites.

With Collins scoring a team-high 32 points, the Olympians won in Greensboro, 82-76. Collins still has a picture of himself from that night, driving against Julius Erving. "To play that well against a team of NBA All-Stars, that really showed I had gotten to the next level," Collins said. Closing out the series on August 16, this time against a joint squad of NBA and ABA players, the Olympians won yet again, 76-65. The five victories boosted the young Olympians, particularly those who had broken out with their play. Tom Henderson was one of them. "They knew by the end of the game who I was," he said.

Still, the team had its skeptics. After playing the Olympians in Louisville, Cleveland Cavaliers guard Butch Beard confessed, "I think they may be in trouble. They didn't have too much trouble with us, but they're going to have trouble with Russia. This isn't the same team we had in '68, that's for sure." Another NBA player, Clem Haskins, said he thought the team was too deliberate on offense and needed to run the ball more.

After the final exhibition game, the team headed to the White House on August 16 for its last U.S. stop before the Games. At the big sendoff at the White House, attended by hundreds of other Olympians, his teammates were astounded to see McMillen, who had been on the President's Council on Physical Fitness and Sports since he was in high school, working the room, seemingly knowing all of the luminaries from different walks of life. Along with the rest of the U.S. Olympic contingent, the team also went to a lunch hosted by Pat Nixon.

Johnny Bach received an unwelcome surprise just before the team was to leave from Munich. The USOC told Iba, unexpectedly, that the team could have only one assistant coach. Haskins, having played for Iba at Oklahoma State, would have been Iba's clear choice, leaving Bach out. For Bach, who was hoping a gold medal in Munich could position him to return in 1976 in Montreal, perhaps as head coach, to be left behind would be devastating, especially after spending the whole summer with the team. Bach lamented all the work he had put in, which was unpaid to boot. Iba went back and told the USOC that Bach had been scouting the Soviet players and was the only one who knew their tendencies, and thus it was critical that he be on the sideline in Munich. Iba also pointed out that Bach had spent 16 years toiling with the Olympic Committee in hopes of becoming an assistant coach. Finally, Iba got hold of Bach: it was okay; he could go. On August 18, the team departed for Munich.

Ed Ratleff greeted by First Lady Pat Nixon and her daughter Julie Nixon at a White House reception prior to the team leaving for Munich. (Courtesy of Herbert J. Mols family).

Part IV

Die Heiteren Spiele (The Serene Games)

Brown was cut from the
final roster and sent home
for R&T while he was
replaced with Walton
and departed for Munich

CHAPTER 20

In the Shadow of the Berlin Games

Leni Riefenstahl's notorious Nazi propaganda film *Olympia,* which idealized the Berlin Summer Olympics of 1936, may be one of the most frightening works of art ever made. It dramatizes exactly how Hitler's government used the Games to advance its guiding principle of Aryan racial supremacy, and in so doing foretold what a Germany-conquered Europe might have looked like had things turned out differently in World War II.

Riefenstahl, a popular German actress in the 1920s and '30s who had become "Hitler's filmmaker," filled her frames with young German athletes swimming, diving and sprinting their way to the most gold medals of any nation in the 1936 Olympics. She captured the fascist grandeur of the twin stone clock towers that highlight the spanking new, partially Albert Speer–designed Olympic Stadium, the "ruin value" of which was intended to glorify the founding fathers of the Third Reich for centuries to come. (If Riefenstahl was the Nazi house filmmaker, Speer was the Nazi house architect from a well-to-do, aristocratic German family; he would later be sentenced at the Nuremberg war crimes tribunals to 20 years in prison.) Riefenstahl's adoring tour with her camera throughout swastika-festooned Berlin followed a young blond runner, the last of some 3,000 youths from seven nations who carried the Olympic flame across Europe from the temple of Zeus to Berlin. When the torch bearer entered the stadium, tens of thousands gave the Nazi salute in unison as Hitler opened the Games. The subsequent release of 3,000 white doves serves, in retrospect, as grim irony.

Adding to the ugliness of the opening ceremony, athletes from many countries turned to acknowledge the German Führer, watching from his podium, with "Heil Hitler" salutes. Other delegations did what they could to undermine the spectacle. The New Zealand athletes ingeniously gave a full salute but "accidentally" acknowledged an obscure Hitler functionary who was standing far to the left of the Führer and his entourage. The U.S.

standard-bearer abruptly pulled the Stars and Stripes up higher as the U.S. delegation passed Hitler, rather than engaging in the customary lowering of the flag in deference to the host country's leader. The U.S. flag was the only one that did not get lowered as it passed Hitler. Riefenstahl may have been a Nazi apologist and master propagandist, but even her many critics have noted her eye for the revealing detail, and in capturing that moment she was more documentary journalist than Nazi apparatchik.

The U.S. would continue to defy Hitler at the 1936 Games. Jesse Owens famously won four gold medals, beating several Germans in the process. Then there was basketball, making its debut as an Olympic sport. The Americans bested the German team by the unbelievable and, from a sportsmanship perspective, unconscionable score of 130-8. The U.S. likely had every intention of handing the Germans any embarrassing defeat it could.

Many Americans, in fact, thought that the U.S. should have refused to attend the Berlin Olympics. At the very least, Hitler's barring of Jews who qualified for the German national team violated clearly defined Olympic bylaws. Avery Brundage of Chicago was the head of the USOC in the mid-1930s and a true believer in the modern Olympic movement as defined by Frenchman Baron Pierre de Coubertin, whose efforts to restart the Games were realized with the 1896 Athens Summer Games. De Coubertin envisioned the Olympics as an oasis of amateur athleticism, untouched by professionalism and set high above the inevitable national rivalries of any given era. Brundage embraced this philosophy that nations' geopolitical or military ambitions fell outside the purview of the Olympics. Even the existence of regimes such as Hitler's Germany—by 1933, Jews were already being herded to Dachau, the Nazis' first concentration camp—couldn't dissuade Brundage from his worldview. All he cared about was whether a host country could build the facilities and transportation arteries to deliver the Games as promised. Brundage, therefore, rejected calls for a U.S. boycott of the 1936 Olympics.

Thirty years later, West Germany (officially the Federal Republic of Germany) was at a crossroads, still under the shadow of World War II. As officials from the Bavarian capital of Munich considered their bid for the 1972 Summer Olympic Games, they kept in mind one simple credo: a potential Munich Games must be the polar opposite of the Berlin Games in every way imaginable. Such sensitivity was perfectly understandable from a German national standpoint, of course, but for the city of Munich the stakes were even higher and the wound from the Nazi years even deeper.

Munich, after all, had given birth to the Nazis. It was there that Hitler, still casting about for his calling in the early 1920s after failing as an artist in Vienna, became involved with a militant, disaffected group of radicals that he transformed into the Nazi party. It was in Munich that Hitler attempted his "beer hall putsch" in November 1923, and it was in a Bavarian prison Hitler wrote his repugnant autobiography, *Mein Kampf*, the work in which he memorialized his hatred of the Jews, theororized on Germany's overlooked "Jewish peril," and warned of the coming Jewish effort to gain world domination. It was on the outskirts of Munich that Dachau opened its gates in 1933.

Just as the Munich organizers wanted to expunge the stain of Nazism from their city, so, too, did West German Chancellor Willy Brandt. He called Munich 1972 a chance to "showcase modern Germany" and replace memories of the Berlin Games with the "Die Heiteren Spiele," or "Serene Games," which became the official motto of the event. Erich Segal, a classicist, novelist and marathon runner who helped broadcast the Games for U.S. television and French radio, would later write that attaching such a moniker to the Games years before a single medal had been awarded was a peculiar kind of "arrogant self-effacement." But there was no questioning West Germany's enthusiasm. The Munich Olympics Organizing Committee, in perhaps setting its own Olympic record, took just one month in 1965 to secure from Brandt's government and the taxpayers of Munich a promise of funding for the Games.

In their bid, Munich organizers said their Games would reflect the open, laid-back and festive atmosphere of the new Munich, with its art galleries, cafes and historic architecture. In his missive to the IOC announcing that Munich would compete for the Games, its mayor wrote that staging the Games there "would unite the youth of the world in the true spirit of the original Olympic idea. . . .We would make every effort to see to it that the art-loving city of Munich offers Olympic Games of extraordinary beauty which would have its special characteristic in uniting bodily and spiritual development." Olympic historian Christopher Clark Elzey describes Munich in the late 1960s and early 1970s as: "one of Europe's most pleasant places to live. The economy was humming along ... Affable and pleasant, Munich was new Germany's poster child ... One could just as easily visit a museum gallery and contemplate a Rembrandt or a Rubens as one could appreciate a good beer garden bonhomie."

When the time came to choose the host for the 1972 Summer Games, Brundage had been the head of the IOC for more than a decade, and the Munich Olympics was to be the last over which he would preside. After final presentations from officials representing four finalists—Detroit, Montreal, Madrid and Munich—Brundage announced from Rome's Excelsior Hotel on April 27, 1968, that the '72 Summer Games belonged to Munich. From that moment on, everything possible was done by the Munich organizing committee to plan an Olympic program completely devoid of the Teutonic nationalism and pageantry of Hitler's Olympics.

No detail was too small to attend to if it would accentuate the difference between Germany of 1936 and Germany of 1972. One of the first decisions the committee made was to embrace a pastel color scheme that would promote a decidedly '60s, peace-loving, "New Age" vibe. Stark black and red hues were not to be used in the Munich Olympics communications or advertising. Soon enough, the organizers had come up with the cute and cuddly Waldi, the first official Olympic mascot. It didn't matter to officials if their Games came off a little silly; the Third Reich didn't do silly.

1972 Opening ceremony, Munich, Germany. (Courtesy of Herbert J. Mols family).

CHAPTER 21
The Team Arrives in Germany

Very few of the U.S. basketball players had families or friends who could afford to travel to Munich to see the Games. The exceptions were Doug Collins's fiancée, Tom Burleson's fiancée, Kenny Davis's wife, Kevin Joyce's mother, Tom McMillen's father and his college coach, Lefty Driesell. The first thing the team did, along with the entire U.S. Olympic contingent, was visit Dachau, an excursion arranged by their hosts. According to Bach, even the players who didn't know or care a thing about history or World War II were moved as they toured the concentration camp.

Players arriving at Munich Airport prior to the opening ceremony. (Courtesy of Herbert J. Mols family).

But just as in Colorado, where the players had no time to hike in the mountains, and in Hawaii, where they had no time for the beach, in Munich the team spent little time touring the city. In fact, the only real day trips they would make were to the CIA facility where they practiced. Iba feared the Soviets and other teams would spy on their practices at the Basketballhalle, where the games would be held and where each team was expected to hold its workouts. He told Bach and Haskins that he "didn't trust the damn Russians." After working with the team all summer on their motion offense and multiple passing schemes, Iba was adamant that he didn't want to give anything away. So instead of setting up a practice schedule for the arena, Iba procured a gym about a 50-mile drive away from Munich at a secure CIA base. Adding to the skulduggery, a police escort would accompany the team there and back. This meant the players were travelling round-trip 100 miles each day to get in a simple practice, plenty of time for Iba to snack on the bouillon and half-sandwiches he preferred for an early lunch. From the trials at the Air Force Academy to the three-week camp at Pearl Harbor to the Olympic practices at the CIA installation, Iba nurtured the military subtext throughout his team's preparation.

The CIA court was first-rate, and the secrecy was of the strictest nature—perfect for Iba. The team bus had to pass through a number of checkpoints and gates. "If you think a submarine base is protected," Bach says, "you should have seen this place." But even Bach thought the idea of holding practices at an undisclosed CIA base was rather silly.

"What could the Russians learn by watching us?" Bach asked Iba at one point.

"They could see the lanes of our passing game," Iba replied matter of factly.

"But there are so many, I don't even know them," Bach said. "You are the only one who knows them."

The opening ceremonies took place on August 26 under a brutal sun. The U.S. basketball players were nattily turned out in red, white and blue suits, as were all of the American male athletes. They were broiling under the stands as they waited their turn to march out onto the stadium track. The musical contrast with the Berlin opening ceremonies was obvious. In Berlin, the athletes practically goose-stepped to military-inspired marches. In

Munich, the teams processed to a low-key composition by Kurt Edelhagen, a German jazz musician, who had blended the musical traditions of all 121 participating nations into a single work.

The basketball players may not recall that the 584-member U.S. delegation entered the Olympic Stadium to Edelhagen's interpretation of "When the Saints Go Marching In," but none has forgotten the releasing of the white doves and the resulting mess they left on unsuspecting athletes. Kevin Joyce remembers how veteran Olympians from the U.S. and other countries knew to take cover under newspapers they'd packed for just this reason. "I remember standing in the infield, all of the athletes lined up by country," Joyce said. "As soon as the doves were released, they pooped on everybody."

USA delegation outside the Olympic stadium about to enter for the opening ceremony (Courtesy of the Herbert J. Mols family).

The players, despite their schedules, did get to enjoy some downtime in the Olympic Village, which in keeping with the intention of the organizers was, by all accounts, offered a wonderful atmosphere for the athletes. The American basketball players noticed immediately the easy-going, baby blue–uniformed security guards. In another equal-and-opposite reaction to the Berlin Games, the 20,000 guards were unarmed. As an indication of the guards' degree of professionalism, Mike Bantom went on a couple of dates with one of them. "There was almost no security in the Olympic village," Bantom said. "Their idea of security was a bunch of college students wearing blue uniforms."

102

Jim Brewer, though, does remember that in addition to the legions of young guards, there was a sprinkling of Munich police officers and West German Army soldiers, who were used more as drivers than anything else. "What I recall is that the Germans were very big on uniforms," Brewer said. But not so big on actual security, at least not at the "Serene Games."

Hank Iba knew he couldn't exert his authority in the Olympic Village, where the whole idea was that athletes mix with their peers from other countries, so he didn't even try. That meant the players could enjoy the restaurants, game rooms and nightclub. They could wander throughout the Olympic Village and sample the cuisines of the participating countries. Joyce recalled the first few days in the Village as "a lot of fun with all the other athletes and trading pins and things like that." He added: "Your family could come in and hang out. There was a disco in there. It was basically a city for us. The restaurants were open all the time." According to Doug Collins, his fiancée, Kathy, would just flash his photo ID and the security guards would casually let her in. Collins, with his USA warm-ups on, was obviously an athlete, so he just strolled in. The lack of security, to the American players, at that point made the whole experience more enjoyable.

Athletes' residence in the Olympic Village. (Courtesy of Herbert J. Mols family).

The truth was that the coaches were also enjoying the Olympic Village. Bach, who had served on various Olympic committees but never before attended the Games, was enjoying the experience immensely. "You needed a map there was so many parts of the Village," Bach said. "You could eat whatever food you wanted. If you wanted Egyptian food you could get

Egyptian food. It was that kind of freedom." Bach also noted that with the excellent Munich Metro, one could be downtown in minutes. Although the coaches didn't venture out much, Bach remembers Iba's throwing a big dinner for the team's staff at an iconic Munich restaurant.

According to Jim Forbes, there were some unspoken ground rules for the black players at the Munich Games. Four years earlier, the sprinters Tommie Smith and John Carlos had made their black power salute on the medal stand in Mexico City. Forbes respected Carlos and Smith because, he said, their actions "took an awful lot of courage." The two athletes, he said, "paid a price for it, but they felt it was worth it. Whether you agreed or disagreed with them, they took a stand." Forbes was correct that there were lingering fears within the USOC about a similar demonstration being made in Munich.

In fact, a good number of the U.S. athletes had already taken a political stand leading up to the Games. Rhodesia, which like South Africa practiced apartheid at that time, had been granted the right to participate in the Games if the team marched under the flag of its former colonial settler, Great Britain. This prompted several contingents of black athletes from various countries, including the United States, to announce they would not compete if Rhodesia were allowed to participate. Avery Brundage, the IOC president, staying consistent with his belief that the Olympics transcended politics, insisted Rhodesia had every right to send a team. The delegates of the IOC, however, voted Rhodesia out of the Games just days before the events were to begin. Brundage was furious, yet he had no choice but to announce that the Rhodesians were not allowed to compete. The vote against Rhodesia tore at the heart of the Olympic ideal Brundage held dear. With Munich being his last Olympics before he gave way to the new head of the IOC, Brundage couldn't imagine anything worse happening to close out his tenure.

Though none of the American basketball players protested Rhodesia's inclusion—anyone foolhardy enough to do so would likely have been handed a one-way plane ticket home—Forbes thought the black athletes in Munich were viewed with slight suspicion by the powers that be. "As a black athlete," Forbes said, "I was never directly told" not to demonstrate for racial justice, "but I'm sure that crossed some of those committee members' minds."

CHAPTER 22
Let the Games Begin

Compared with that of the Pan Am Games the year before, FIBA's draw for the basketball competition at the Munich Olympics was the height of transparency. The 16 qualifying teams were split into two groups, with the top-seeded Americans and Soviets each heading a different half of the draw. A quick look at the draw reveals the U.S. received the tougher half. Both Brazil and Cuba, the nation that had beaten the U.S. in international competition just a year earlier, were in the same division as the U.S. In the Soviet division were Puerto Rico, led by U.S. collegiate coach Gene Bartow, and Yugoslavia, a dangerous team but not at the level of Brazil and Cuba.

The 6,500-seat Basketballhalle was about four and a half miles south of the Olympic village. Even on days when the U.S. didn't have a game Bach made the shuttle-bus trip to the arena to scout the other teams. Sometimes Iba and Haskins went with him. The coaches were sufficiently worried about the Cuban team that all three watched the Cubans play its opening game. But a rout by Cuba led to its star Pedro Chappe, who repeatedly burned the Americans the year before in Colombia, playing only a few minutes before being rested.

The Americans played their first game against Czechoslovakia. The opening minutes served as a reminder—despite the international rise of basketball and the legitimate threats from Cuba, Brazil and the Soviet Union—of just how far the U.S. basketball program was ahead of most other nations. The Americans overplayed the passing lanes, making every trip down court an adventure for the Czechs. Bobby Jones, Doug Collins, Tom Henderson and Kevin Joyce harassed the Czechs into turnover after turnover. Dwight Jones repeatedly hit his feathery turnaround jumper in the lane, showing why he was such a force in Texas high school basketball and why such big things were expected from him at the University of Houston. Joyce nailed tough shots off the dribble.

Henderson, Iba's personal pick for the team, made the aging coach seem like a genius even before the first half was over. As Henderson dashed through the Czech defense as if he were back on the blacktop of New York City playgrounds, it was clear that the San Jacinto Junior College graduate would serve as the floor general for this team of much more highly acclaimed players. Bill Russell, the legendary Boston Celtics center, worked the Olympics as a commentator along with Frank Gifford, the former New York Giants star running back who had recently made a smooth transition to the broadcasting booth. Russell pointed out that the unheralded Henderson was the best player on the floor for the U.S., and that Iba deserved credit for picking him.

Frank Gifford interviewing Hank Iba after the Czechoslovakia game with Bill Russell sitting in the background. (Courtesy of Herbert J. Mols family).

Russell's presence at the Games was a big deal for the basketball Olympians, and not just the players on the U.S. squad. Just a few years retired, Russell was the Michael Jordan of his day—a player who refused to lose when the game was on the line. He led the Celtics to 11 NBA titles in his 13-year NBA career, and was happy to do it by playing defense and blocking shots even while his offensive-minded rival, Wilt Chamberlain, piled up obscene scoring stats. Russell "was a huge star in the world," recalled Gifford. "I talked to all the coaches on the U.S. team, and they were mesmerized by Bill Russell."

In Munich, though, Russell sometimes frustrated Gifford and their third boothmate, veteran ABC sportscaster Bill Flemming. Since he was at once both the color-commentating "talent" and the ultimate big man on campus, Russell did not have to overburden himself with preparation. Gifford and Russell though, complemented each other well, especially when they took the telecast beyond basketball. During one game, they talked about the tendency of the Germans to over-engineer, what with built-in electronic alarms in their hotel rooms and buzzers that the coaches held throughout the game and pressed when they wanted a timeout. "It's hard to get in and out of the parking lot without some sort of contraption," Gifford said on air. "And those electronic alarms…You will wake up…You must wake up."

In a postgame interview after the Americans' 66-35 victory over Czechoslavakia, Iba beamed, showering praise on Henderson, who led the team in scoring with 16 points. Iba also singled out Dwight Jones, who had been named captain for the game, as having played particularly well. But most of all, Iba praised his team's defense. For the players, having such an easy first game was almost a letdown after the coaches had been emphasizing all summer how difficult winning the gold medal would be. Bantom remembers the game as a revelation. "What we found out in game number one was that these guys couldn't play and that we were going to kick their butt," Bantom said. "They couldn't run and they couldn't handle our defense."

In its second game, the team won comfortably over Australia, 81-55. Ed Ratleff scored 18 points. To Bach, the game was memorable because he was able to implement his trademark zone defense. Iba asked Bach how good his zone was, because he was thinking of using it. Bach replied, "How good is it? About as good as the five minutes you let me practice it." Not amused, Iba called a timeout anyway and told the team to start playing the zone. Bach pleaded with the players: "Goddamn it guys, you got to make this zone work." It did, and the Americans promptly shut the Aussies down.

With two games behind them, the Americans were also settling into an off-court routine. After walking out for breakfast, they would go to the training room to get taped up and receive treatment for assorted bruises and sore muscles. Then the team would board its bus and embark on the roundtrip odyssey to practice. In the afternoon it was back to the village for some rest. On game days the team would have an early meal and head for the arena. On other days the team had time to mingle with other athletes. The Soviet and Cuban athletes seemed hostile toward the Americans' overtures. Several times American players tried to introduce themselves, as they did with the athletes representing all the nations, and each time their olive branch was rebuffed.

The highly athletic Cubans, however, certainly weren't afraid of engaging *on* the court. Coming off their 73-69 win over the U.S. at the Pan Am Games—albeit against a team that included only Dwight Jones, Jim Forbes and Kenny Davis from the U.S. squad in Munich—the Cubans fielded essentially the same lineup, and expected to do well. As added motivation—for both teams, actually—Cuban dictator Fidel Castro had announced he would fly to Munich to personally decorate the Cuban basketball players if they beat the United States. For the U.S., after two routs, the question was whether the team would have any trouble going toe-to-toe in an emotional game. Just to be sure, Iba, not one for unnecessary motivational speeches, stood at the door of the locker room as the team was about to take the court. Castro's promise, posted on a bulletin board for all of the American players and coaches to see, had fired up Iba. He gave a simple, chilling message: "Let the damn blood run."

Dwight Jones, who played the first half as if he desired personal redemption for the previous year's loss to Cuba, powered the U.S. to a 13-3 lead and finished with 18 points as the Americans won going away, 67-48. It was the 58th straight Olympic victory for the U.S. basketball team. After the game, Iba was asked whether he thought much about the winning streak. "I think about it," he said. "But I don't talk about it." The next night, the Americans would go for win number 59 against Brazil, another squad that gave the U.S. fits at the Pan Am Games. Russell predicted the U.S. would have to "really work" to beat the Brazilians.

He couldn't have phrased it better. Brazil's 20-year-old center, Marcos Abdallah, was one of the world's best. Several American players, looking back, called him one of the toughest players in the tournament. The score was tied, 26-26, at the end of the first half, but Brazil was up by seven with 12 minutes left when Abdallah performed a beautiful drop step in the post and had an easy attempt to put Brazil up by nine points—and missed. The U.S. broke the other way, with Henderson converting a layup. Russell commented that the Americans should keep "running the ball down their throats," a not so veiled criticism of Iba's slow-paced style and how it had the U.S. playing in a funk for most of the game.

Joyce nailed one of his patented on-the-move jump shots. Then a Jim Brewer tip-in pulled the U.S. within one before Collins hit a reverse layup to give the Americans the lead, 46-45. But Brazil didn't back down. Abdullah and his teammates fought for every rebound and dove for every loose ball. For the Brazilians, this clearly was their gold medal game. After Abdullah hit the deck for the umpteenth time with about seven minutes left, he shrugged it off, wiped away the blood and sweat and kept playing.

Henderson made a steal and sank two big baskets to put the U.S. up, 53-49. Russell said on air, in what might have been a slap at the absent Walton, that the Americans had "no big star, but they are proving they are not a bunch of nobodies." Faint praise perhaps, but the Americans were playing inspired basketball against an impressive team. Ratleff hit a jumper to make it 55-51, giving them a little breathing room. In fact, Ratleff took complete charge at the end of the game, driving to the basket as if he were dominating the freshmen at Long Beach State. After Brazil again drew within one point, Ratleff hit a leaner in the lane to make it 57-54, and on the next possession he was fouled driving the lane. He made both foul shots, which, combined with a block by Bantom on Abdallah, all but sealed the victory. Ratleff had scored six of the Americans' final eight points in the 61-54 win. In four games, the U.S. already had four or five players emerge as clutch performers.

Even though the U.S. was now 4-0, the Americans didn't seem quite at home with the international rules. Often, they didn't throw the ball in quickly enough on in-bounds plays; under international rules a player didn't have to "check" the ball with the referee. In addition, although goaltending wasn't allowed, it was rarely called in international competition. In the Brazil game Abdulla and his teammates started swatting the Americans' shots away as they descended toward the basket. The U.S. players, on the other hand, never challenged Brazil's shots in this manner; the players were conditioned not to. These are just small examples of how the international veterans had an advantage over their young American opponents—the U.S. didn't know how to traverse the gray areas between international and American rules.

Another way the U.S. didn't take advantage of the rules was in deciding whether or not to take foul shots. International rules at the time stipulated that, during the last three minutes of the second half, all fouls resulted in two free throws—unless the team that was fouled chose not to shoot them. A team could elect to inbound the ball instead, with the goal of running time off the clock, a strategy that would prevent the kind of "hack-a-Shaq" defense at the Games that would years later by played in the NBA on Shaquille O'Neal, a notoriously bad foul shooter. Typically, the U.S. chose to shoot foul shots. Although this strategy wasn't *wrong*, it seemed odd that the coaches wouldn't try something different once or twice, just in case in a game to come the Americans would rather run the clock out than shoot free throws.

In the next game, the U.S. didn't need to apply any of those lessons. The team's rout of Egypt felt like a scrimmage. Bach had scouted the Egyptians a couple of times and told Iba that the Americans could start anyone, in any combination, and still win the game. But in the first minute, an Egyptian player hit consecutive shots to put his team up, 4-0. Iba looked at Bach and said, "Johnny, you better be right." Bach was right: the game was all but over by halftime. The final score: United States 96, Egypt 31.

The team's sixth game, however, proved a revealing contest against Spain (which featured a goaltending call, prompting Russell to say, "I've watched nine games and that's the first goaltending call I've seen made."). For one thing, more evidence came in that, contrary to Iba's master plan of working the ball around for five or six passes to wear out opposing defenses, the U.S. players were at their best when running the floor.

As in the Brazil game, the Americans seemed mired in quicksand early in the game. They were down by five points approaching the first half before a string of steals allowed Henderson and Collins to fast break. A put-back by Bantom made the score 29-28 in favor of the Americans; another layup made it 31-28. Clearly, when the Americans could get out on the break after a steal they were getting easy scoring chances.

Another interesting development occurred just as the U.S. was about to pull away from Spain. With the score 41-36 and their height advantage and defensive quickness starting to take effect, the Americans got a tip-in basket from Bantom. The referee held up two fingers for the universal indication of a made basket worth two points. But as the Spaniards brought the ball up the court, Gifford, as well as the referees, noticed at virtually the same time that the U.S. hadn't been given credit for the basket.

As Iba, Bach, Haskins and the referees all converged at the scorer's table, Gifford and Russell assumed the obvious mistake would be rectified immediately. But after a couple of minutes of discussion, there was still no credit given for the basket. The American coaches walked away befuddled. Gifford quizzically observed that "the scorer overruled the referee ... I guess we'll never know." He added, "We have seen some strange calls this week.' Such odd calls, miscommunications with the scorer's table, and strange innovations such as the coach's timeout buzzer were all aspects of the competition that seemed fairly harmless halfway through the tournament. But they would prove to haunt the Americans in the end.

The U.S. finished off Spain, 72-56, to get to 6-0 in the tournament, clinching a spot in the semifinals. One last preliminary game remained, against Japan, a contest which on paper would be the Americans' easiest matchup of all. "Some of those teams at that time were terrible," said Bobby Knight. "I mean, they couldn't play dead."

Johnny Bach relished the Japan game. The 27 years since the end of World War II and the emergence of Japan as one of the U.S.'s main allies and trading partners didn't mean Bach had forgiven the war in the Pacific, which had claimed his brother's life. Urging the team to pile on the points against the "Japs," Bach and the other coaches never let up. At one point, after Japan scored on successive trips down court, Iba replaced several players with others "who wanted to play defense," as he put it. If there was ever a 99-33 game that wasn't as close as the score indicates, this was it. Seven of the Americans scored in double figures, with McMillen and Dwight Jones leading with 14 points apiece.

Meanwhile, the Soviets were holding up their end, showing off an extremely potent offense that was leading the tournament in scoring. As the U.S. rolled over Japan and Egypt, the Soviet Union enjoyed laughers against Senegal (94-52) and Poland (94-64), a team which, as a Soviet Bloc nation, probably wasn't *allowed* to win the game. The Soviets also manhandled West Germany, 87-63, before playing a slightly closer game with Italy, 79-66. After a win against Puerto Rico, 100-87, in a game that saw the star forward Aleksandr Belov explode for 37 points, followed by a rout of the Philippines, the Soviets finally faced a test in the preliminary round, a tough 74-67 win over Yugoslavia. All in all, though, the Soviets never had a result that was really in doubt, whereas the U.S. played three games it could have lost.

Bill Summers, Don Haskins, Hank Iba, Johnny Bach and Herb Mols (Courtesy of Herbert J. Mols family).

CHAPTER 23
The Snakebit Americans

As the basketball tournament unfolded, there were many other story lines to the Olympics. Mark Spitz and his demolition of numerous swimming records—he liked to show off his medals around the Olympic village—were the talk of the Games the same way Michael Phelps would be at the Beijing Olympics in 2008. Olga Korbet, a Soviet gymnast, somersaulted and vaulted into the hearts of everyone, including many Americans who marvelled that a Soviet athlete could show real emotion and vulnerability. Still, to Americans watching back home, there seemed to be in Munich—if not anti-Americanism on the part of the officials—a startling amount of bad officiating that kept costing the U.S. gold medals.

In boxing, a 21-year old American light-middleweight named Reggie Jones seemingly was cruising, doing everything but knocking his Soviet opponent through the ropes and out of the ring. Jones, by all accounts, landed far more punches than his opponent did in the gold medal bout. But he lost on points, prompting the crowd to throw trash into the ring after the decision was announced.

Granted, boxing judges are notorious for their inconsistent scoring. But then there was the diving competition. After a series of questionable scores for American divers, the USOC filed a formal protest with international diving officials, which went nowhere. In gymnastics, American Cathy Rigby received such low scores for a strong performance that one U.S. coach decried that numerous communist judges were guilty of "the biggest rape of justice in athletics."

One of most controversial decisions cost 16-year-old swimming phenom Rick DeMont the gold medal he had won while shattering the world record in the 1,500-meter freestyle. After his incredible performance, DeMont tested positive for a banned substance that was commonly found in asthma medicine. DeMont had reported his usage of the drug on a questionnaire prior to the Games, but his coaches never realized he shouldn't be taking it. He had to forfeit his medal, and his family would never forgive the USOC or the U.S. swimming coaches.

The track and field competition also had several dramas involving Americans. Two track athletes, Vince Matthews and Wayne Collett, who did no more than slouch during their own national anthem, were banished from the Games for the rest of their lives after their—in the words of Brundage—"disgusting behavior." Matthews and Collett were the gold- and silver-medal winners, respectively, in the 400 meters. The crowd booed and the international media excoriated the two runners, but the level of vitriol far exceeded the offense. These were two young men who had just fulfilled a lifelong dream and then acted a bit too casually during their historic moment.

But, clearly, their lackadaisical personas on the medal stand did not represent a planned show of defiance in the manner of Smith's and Carlos's gloved fists four years earlier. It was more like bad table manners on the part of a dinner guest. Poor form, certainly, but not a reason to bar the guest from one's home in perpetuity. The runners' expulsion from the Munich Olympics and any future Games, in fact, seemed to illustrate the hair-trigger state of the IOC after the Rhodesia fiasco. Indeed, whereas Smith and Carlos were sent home, Matthews and Collett were given what amounted to a career death penalty.

The American track team also suffered from another self-inflicted debacle. Incredibly, two U.S. favorites for gold in the 100-meter dash, Eddie Hart and Rey Robinson, were disqualified when they failed to appear for their second-round qualifying heat. One of the team's coaches, Stan Wright, took the blame, admitting that he had told the athletes the qualifying heat would be run later in the day. Hart noted that he couldn't read German and, because he wanted to concentrate on his events, he didn't read any English-language newspapers while at the Games either.

In addition, a far more decorated American athlete was also taken to task in Munich. Mark Spitz was nearly expelled for inadvertently displaying his Adidas shoes in the midst of his record-setting binge of seven gold medals. According to a document from the Olympic archives in the IOC library in Lausanne, Spitz apologized in order to stay in Munich and continue competing. One of Brundage's nods to amateurism was to punish anyone he felt was brazenly promoting his or her athletic sponsor. In his excitement after winning his third gold medal, Spitz said in his letter: "I picked up my shoes to put them on and was photographed as I unconsciously waved greetings to the crowds with the hand in which I was holding my shoes, my other hand and arm being wrapped around my fellow athlete." He explained that Dr. Harold Henning, honorary secretary of the international amateur swimming association, had paraded Spitz and other medal winners around the pool and advised them to show their appreciation for the crowd.

Although Spitz was ultimately allowed to pursue his assault on the record books, the fact that he even had to write such a letter of explanation for simply waving to the crowd was absurd. The pattern of poor judging and rulings against U.S. athletes enraged many Americans at home watching on television. The Olympic Museum archives in Lausanne are replete with thousands of letters from Americans outraged at these and other perceived slights borne by the American athletes in Munich, some whom were starting to wonder whether anger over the Vietnam War and the unpopularity of President Nixon in Europe were creating a decidedly anti-American bias.

CHAPTER 24

One Day in September

On Tuesday, September 5, 1972, about two-thirds of the way through the Games, the U.S. team was preparing for its semifinal against Italy and the Soviet Union was to play Cuba. From Rhodesia's ejection from the Games to DeMont's gold medal forfeiture to the many judging controversies, the Serene Games were turning out to be anything but serene. But soon all of those snafus would seem as important as the sandbox disputes of children. The Games were about to be marred by one of the most notorious terrorist attacks in history.

At some point during the first week of the Games, a scouting trip was made into the Olympic Village, but it had nothing to do with any athletic contest. A man and a woman, operatives from an obscure terrorist group that called itself Black September, entered the Village and sized up one of the identical buildings to Building 31 Connollystrasse, the three-story dorm that housed the Israeli delegation. How the pair got past the gates without a badge is unclear, but given the lax security, they could have talked their way in. "There wasn't any security out where the public walked," Bantom said. "We went in and out of the village all the time; all you had to do was show your badge and you walked through."

Black September's plan was to storm the Israeli dormitory and hold the athletes hostage in exchange for Israel's release of more than two hundred Palestinian prisoners. Although Israel's longstanding refusal to negotiate with terrorists was well-known, later scholarship on the attack indicates the terrorists believed Israel might soften its stance given that the hostages were beloved athletes at the most high-profile event in the world. It's impossible to know whether Black September targeted the Games because they were aware of the West Germans' commitment to an open, welcoming event. But the lack of real security surely contributed to the terrorists' ability to plan and execute the attack.

In the early morning of September 5, nine men, dressed in Adidas warm-up suits to look like athletes, took cabs to the Olympic Village. The terrorist team knew that many athletes, rather than hoof it all the way back to the front entrance of the Village, would scale the 10-foot-high chain-link fence that encircled the village. This practice was not uncommon among the American basketball players. Dwight Jones remembers climbing the fence after being out late one night in Munich. "We saw they had closed the gate for getting in, and we climbed the fence," Jones said. Brewer, too, remembers players not bothering to use the main entrance, instead slipping in and out of the Village after hours via the surrounding fence. Brewer also recalls that the final construction of the Olympic Village had finished just days before the Games, leaving a chaotic work-site feel to the whole area.

But on the night the terrorists snuck in, it probably wasn't the Americans who helped them over the fence. Ever since the last surviving Black September terrorist said in the 1999 documentary One Day in September that a group of Americans helped the terrorists negotiate the fence, it's been accepted as fact. But a group of Canadian athletes recently stepped forward and told the Toronto Star that it was they, coming back from watching a Canada-Soviet "Hockey Summit" game, who had helped the Palestinians over the fence. The Canadians were staying in the dorm next to Building 31 and often scaled the fence themselves rather than walk all the way around to the main entrance. Canadian water polo players Robert Thompson and David Hart, and two others from Hamilton, Ontario, confirmed to the paper in April 2012 that they remembered helping the strange crew of athletes over, and that—like their group—these people had been drinking. "They had to have come over with us," said Thompson. "We assumed they were just other athletes." Hart noted that international travellers often mistake Canadians for Americans. "It's possible there was an American or two in the group, but the vast majority of us were Canadians," Hart said. Speaking of the terrorists, he said, "How would they have known the difference?"

Whether Americans or Canadians or both, the group helped the terrorists in, even willingly accepting their tote bags filled with AKM assault rifles and Tokarev pistols and setting them down on the ground on the other side of the fence. As the tipsy Canadians went on their way, the terrorists made their way to the Israelis' dorm.

It was about 4 AM when the terrorists walked through the unlocked front door of Building 31 Connollystrasse. Their scouting trip days earlier had been fruitful: the terrorists knew exactly which room was farthest from the front door of the dorm, so they would use that one to hold the hostages once they were rounded up. First, the terrorists broke down the door of one of the first-floor corner apartments, killing a wrestling coach and a weightlifter as the two tried to resist. Before being shot to death, the weightlifter, a Six-Day War veteran named Yossef Romano, managed to attack and injure one of the terrorists.

At least two Israelis escaped on foot while, for some reason, the Palestinians overlooked an entire ground-floor room full of Israeli athletes. They, too, escaped. Still, nine Israelis and coaches were rounded up and put in the corner, ground-floor room. The corpse of wrestling coach Moshe Weinberg was left in the room with them. While the rest of the Olympic Village slept, West German police made their way to Building 31 after a report of gunfire inside the building. One of the terrorists handed the police Black September's list of demands.

The U.S. delegation was staying across a courtyard from Building 31, a couple of hundred yards away, as most of the players recall. At one point in the middle of the night, Tommy Burleson and Bobby Jones heard what they assumed were firecrackers being set off. They didn't think any more of it.

For Doug Collins, the first indication that something was terribly wrong came when he left the U.S. team's dormitory to get breakfast with Ed Ratleff, his best friend on the team. After a few steps, Collins spied a group of men—wielding machine guns and wearing black ski masks—on the terrace of the Israelis' dorm. From that distance a sniper would have been easily close enough to pick off Collins and Ratleff. At that point, no one had been told anything, and the U.S. building had not been secured. Collins and Ratleff promptly made a U-turn and ducked back into the dorm.

At about the same time, the usual routine was going on in the training room of the American basketball team. One player was up on the table getting taped, others were milling around waiting their turns. But this time the routine was different. When Bantom entered the room he heard someone say: "Somebody got shot last night. There's police over there right now, and they're guarding the area."

Before the team members knew it, police brandishing automatic weapons surrounded Building 31. Tanks and soldiers streamed into the Village. The young blue-shirted security guards with their smiles and lax attitudes were nowhere to be found. Said Kenny Davis: "I thought we were in the safest and most secure place in the world. After that, nobody was able to leave or get in." Tom McMillen, who had started to play better toward the end of the tournament and was looking forward to the semifinal against Italy, felt as if the bottom had dropped out of the Games. "I've never gone from so high to so low in my life," McMillen said. "It was very surreal seeing these policemen with automatic weapons running through the Village in sweat suits."

Indeed, instead of serving as proud caretakers of the "Serene Games," Olympic officials suddenly found themselves authorizing the presence of tanks and soldiers in the Olympic Village. What had been a celebration of international fellowship had turned into an armed camp. But IOC chief Avery Brundage didn't want to cause panic among the athletes and send them running for the exits. To avoid just that situation, Brundage ordered that the Games go on, even as Mark Spitz and other non-Israeli Jewish athletes were quietly spirited out of the Village for the rest of the Games. Until mid-afternoon, scheduled contests were played, meaning that even while one Israeli athlete and one coach lay dead and nine others were in deathly fear for their lives, other athletes were out winning medals.

The horror of what was occurring was made all the worse because the attack had targeted Jews in the first German Olympics since Berlin, a fact that Brundage seemed oblivious to as he ordered the Games to continue. Erich Segal, the Jewish writer and marathon runner who helped broadcast the Games for U.S. television and French radio, had mixed with many of the Israeli athletes before and during the Olympics. In a long article he wrote for The *New York Times* just weeks after the conclusion of the Games, he described the uneasy jocularity of Jewish athletes heading to Munich for the Olympics, and the heartbreak he felt seeing these unspoken fears end up being realized. "Whenever Jews met during the early pre-Olympic euphoria, there were still nervous jokes about watching out in the shower rooms, et cetera," Segal wrote. "It was to exorcise ghosts. Gas chamber humor." Eventually the outrage expressed by numerous national delegations and certain quarters of the media became too much even for the out-of-touch Brundage, who was finally shamed into halting all competition.

As for the American basketball players, they were disbelieving of what had happened and unsure what to do. McMillen says the USOC was fearful of a second wave of attacks. But most of the players recall feeling no fear whatsoever, as it was clear that the terrorists, as nearby as they were, had targeted just the Israelis. "I wasn't afraid because the terrorists didn't want any black guys," Tom Henderson said. "They didn't want us. They'd been fighting for hundreds of years. They talk about being religious and all. I don't get that part." Even so, during the short time that the team was in the dorm during the ordeal, the police told them to stay down and away from the windows. All morning they could see up close what would become one hauntingly iconic image of the 1970s, a lone, armed and masked terrorist perched on the balcony of the neighboring building.

The U.S. ballplayers milled around, wondering whether the Games would be suspended. Guards appeared on the second floor of the U.S. dorm and at their room doors. The team turned to the live television coverage but no one could understand the German broadcast. Kevin Joyce started listening to the Armed Forces Radio to get the latest information. He would update the group with new developments, even as they were happening right across the courtyard.

Police and security officials wanted the team to stay out of the vicinity of the attack, but for security reasons wouldn't allow Iba to take the team out of Munich for its customary 50-mile bus trip to practice. So the team went to the main arena to practice for the first time. The U.S. bus was stopped by security guards on the way to and from the arena, as it would subsequently be every time the players came into or out of the Village. West German police boarded the bus and checked everybody's card. On the way to practice McMillen and Bach talked about what was on everyone's mind: How could they play basketball now?

After hours of practice that day, the Americans still weren't allowed back into their dorm. Bantom remembers players lying on the gym floor, taking naps. Eventually the Americans were sent back to the dorms via an alternate route. They passed through the parking garage underneath their building, and, according to Bobby Jones, saw the military vehicles lined up to take the hostages and terrorists out of the Olympic Village and to the helicopters that would spirit them to the Munich airport as part of the deal the West German authorities had struck with the terrorists.

Tommy Burleson, the 7-foot-2-inch U.S. center, even claims to have run headlong into the terrorists and the Israeli athletes as they were leaving the Olympic Village through one of the underground tunnels. According to Burleson, he was held up against a wall with a gun placed to his head by a Munich police officer until the group had passed. Burleson says he could hear the Israeli athletes crying.

Dennis Lewin, who produced portions of many Olympics, including the Munich Games, for ABC, remembers how difficult it was to confirm what was happening at the airport. One moment reports of gunfire came in, then word of a burning helicopter. At one point, the Munich police announced the athletes were safe. But Roone Arledge, the head of ABC Sports who had revolutionized coverage of the Olympics by emphasizing the human side of sports, wouldn't let his star anchor, Jim McKay, report any information until it could be verified.

Later that night it was confirmed that the remaining nine Israeli athletes and coaches had been killed in an airport shootout between West German police and the terrorists (five of the eight of them were killed as well). The haunting, emotional commentary by McKay is still remembered by legions who watched the broadcast that evening: "Our worst fears have been realized tonight . . . two athletes were killed yesterday in their rooms, nine were killed at the airport. They're all gone."

CHAPTER 25

In the Aftermath of a Terrorist Attack

The Olympics were in chaos. "Our first reaction was just to go home," Mike Bantom said. "It was just scary the way the German police handled everything. It was bad enough that these guys came in and kidnapped these folks and were going to kill them, but then the German solution seemed to be to shoot everybody. It's like, well, this is crazy. We need to get the hell out of here."

Like Bantom, many of the players felt the Games had spun out of control, that the German police couldn't be trusted, and that the competition had lost any semblance of importance. "I think if you'd taken a poll, the results would have been we'd go home," Kenny Davis said.

There were many who agreed. In a column headlined "The Show Goes On," the legendary Red Smith wrote in the *New York Times* on the day of the memorial that perhaps the world's second experiment with the Olympic Games should end. Much as the ancient Olympic Games were abandoned when in the third century A.D. people stopped having faith in the cult of Zeus, Smith mused that the modern Games, too, had outlived their usefulness. "The fact is, these global clambakes have an irresistible attraction as forums for ideological, social or racial expression," Smith wrote. "For this reason, they may have outgrown their britches. Perhaps in the future, it will be advisable to substitute separate world championships . . . which could be conducted in a less hysterical climate." Decades later, when the United States maintained as one of its main foreign policy tenets a belief that terrorists should be pursued all over the world, it would seem fantastical that anyone would have rewarded a terrorist organization by cancelling the Games. But many in 1972 thought the Olympics had become too much of a target.

The only opinion that really counted, though, was Brundage's. His final Games as leader of the IOC had fallen into absolute calamity. His entire set of cherished beliefs—that the Olympics stood on a pedestal well above the Machiavellian world of politics; that the Games were a refuge never to be touched by cruelty or violence—had been confined to the dustbin of history. A terrorist attack on his watch had killed 11 Israeli athletes and coaches. The tragic irony wasn't lost on Doug Collins. "You think of the Olympics as putting all our differences aside and having this competition to bring out the best in each other," Collins said. "Then, at that point, the reality set in. This to me was really a rude awakening that the Cold War was going on and that terrorism and all this stuff was real in our world."

Brundage could bow to the pressure coming from within and beyond the Olympic movement to cancel the rest of the Games, or he could stick to his ideals at a time when, for once, he was clearly on the side of the righteous.

It turned out that, almost three decades before the 9/11 terrorist attacks on the United States, letting terrorists dictate the course of events was indeed anathema to a civilized society. Brundage announced that tickets for the next day's track and field events would instead be honored as tickets for a memorial service for the Israeli dead. The event was to be held in the same stadium that had rung in the Twentieth Olympiad 11 days earlier. There also would be a wreath-laying ceremony at Building 31. The Games would resume on September 7.

Many athletes, including several of the American basketball players, disagreed with the decision. Said Bobby Jones: "I had no desire to play basketball. I was sure they would cancel the Olympics. I'm not a guy to show emotion when someone dies, but in this situation it was different because they were fellow athletes. I think it affected us all a great deal."

But Tom McMillen believes that the much-criticized Brundage finally got one right when he made that decision. "In retrospect, I think it would have been a mistake to cancel the Games because it would have played into the hands of the terrorists," McMillen said. "It would have been a terrible precedent to cancel the Olympics."

For Collins, it was the memorial service that made the difference. "We were obviously all devastated," he recalled. "It was hard because there was that part of us that said, you know, we have come this close and we'd love to be able to finish the Games, and then there was that part of us that wanted to show respect for these athletes who had lost their lives. I think the healing process started when we went to the memorial service and got a chance to pay our respect." Kenny Davis added that, "Looking back on it, I think Avery Brundage was right. He stopped the Games temporarily, everyone paid their respects, but then you have to recover. If he had canceled the games, it would have given the terrorists exactly what they wanted."

Even though 80,000 people attended the memorial, the Soviets were one of the few delegations that did not attend, on orders from Moscow, which meant that Nikolai Avilov, their Jewish decathlon gold medal winner, could not pay his respects. And while Brundage would later be praised for not bowing to the terrorists, he bungled his big moment during the memorial. Still unable to come to terms with his defeat on the Rhodesia question, he spoke during his tribute to the Israeli athletes of "two savage attacks" at the Twentieth Olympiad, one the massacre perpetrated by Black September and the other "the Rhodesia battle." Linking these two events caused universal offense. Brundage's speech was panned, and as far as most everyone was concerned his retirement couldn't come soon enough.

The Americans trounced Italy in the semifinal, 68-38, an eyebrow-raising result given that the Soviets had beaten the Italians by just 13 points. Jim Forbes scored 14 points and Bantom muffled the Italians on defense. The Americans had held their opponents to an amazing 43 points per game in the eight games, justifying Iba's defensive drills that the players had worked on all summer. So far, the Americans had fulfilled Iba's vision of a team composed of interchangeable parts. None of the players was averaging in double figures, but nine were averaging five points or more. Tom Henderson and Dwight Jones led the scoring, averaging about nine points each.

The United States' win over Italy ran the U.S. Olympic basketball record to a perfect 63-0, It was unclear, though, how much Americans back home were supporting the team. Three of the games went completely untelevised and the semifinal against Italy was barely shown. It also was hard to predict, given the chaos of these games, how ABC would present the gold medal game.

As for the Soviets, they ran into more trouble than expected in their semifinal against Cuba. The Soviets trailed, 36-35, at halftime before the Cubans faded the same way they had against the Americans. The Soviets rallied to win by six, 67-61, setting up a Soviet-American final. It was the game the world had been waiting for.

The game could also have a big impact on the final medal standings, a statistic that everyone professes at every Olympics not to care much about but which everyone follows. On the evening of September 9, when the gold medal basketball game was to be played, the United States maintained a seven-medal lead, 81-74, but trailed by four in the number of gold medals, 31-27. All that was needed was a spark to set things off.

Part V

The Game

CHAPTER 26
When Lightning Strikes

The unexpected spark that finally got the Americans going with less than five minutes left in the gold medal game came from the native New Yorker Kevin Joyce. Joyce was staging a mutiny of sorts in the huddle, demanding that Iba let them press and pressure the Soviet players into mistakes. When Iba didn't immediately react to Joyce's urging, Joyce turned to plead his case to assistant coach Johnny Bach. Out of the three coaches, it was Bach who had become closest to the players. Haskins had once played for Iba, and both viewed players as chess pieces to be moved around—and the beauty of chess pieces was that they didn't talk back if they didn't like how they were being used. Bach, on the other hand, was more comfortable with the players as individuals who had opinions and ideas, on the court and off. A case in point was his ill-fated flight over Pearl Harbor with Kenny Davis. The last thing Iba or Haskins ever would have done at Pearl Harbor was invite a player to spend time with him off the court. Bach's connection with the players helped him build their trust. So, when Bach didn't object to the up-tempo plan for the rest of the game, the players were determined to go all out and play a full-court, pressing defense.

Joyce, Collins, Jim Forbes, Henderson and Bantom were the American five who emerged from the huddle with 4:22 left. Brewer checked out of the game for good; he couldn't remember the plays because of the blow to his head. Such circumstances today would call for Brewer's being examined immediately by concussion specialists, but in 1972 he just sat on the bench trying to understand what was going on, peppering Bobby Jones with questions. "When I left the game," Brewer remembered, "I was so frustrated because I couldn't get a grip on the situation. I sat there trying to figure out where the hell I was."

With Brewer and Dwight Jones out of the game, the U.S. team was small by necessity, but actually perfect for what the players had in mind. The scrambling American defense forced a slew of turnovers from the normally sure-handed Soviets. One possession ended up with Sergei Belov's dribbling the ball off his foot and out-of-bounds, a mistake he probably hadn't made since middle school. Meanwhile, Joyce backed up his words during the timeout with six straight points: a drive through the heart of the Soviet defense for a layup, followed by two jumpers. The pro-American crowd rose to its feet.

Don Haskins, Johnny Bach and Hank Iba during the gold medal game. (Courtesy of Johnny Bach).

On the defensive end, the Americans' aggressiveness resulted in several fouls called against them in the backcourt, but the miscues ended up helping the American cause. FIBA rules at the time stipulated that all fouls in the last three minutes of a game sent players to the free throw line unless a team opted to take the ball out of bounds, which seldom happened because of the lure of free points. Turning the final few minutes into a Soviet free throw exhibition turned out to serve two purposes for the Americans. It stopped the clock at every foul, and the Soviets missed several of their free throws.

After Sergei Belov finally converted two foul shots to give the Soviets some breathing room at 49-46, Forbes hit a deep jumper from the right side of the key that hit nothing but net. The U.S. trailed by just a single point, 49-48. On the ensuing play, Sakandelidze was at the point and passed to Paulauskas on the right block. Thirty seconds remained. Paulauskas hit Belov. Back to Paulauskas. Twenty seconds. Paulauskas drove the right baseline and dumped it to Aleksandr Belov, who went up for the chip shot to ice the game. But McMillen, not a leaper and no one's idea of a shock blocker, timed his jump perfectly and stuffed Belov cold. Belov recovered, grabbed the ball, and with 10 seconds left made the fateful decision to try to pass the ball out to Sergei Belov, hovering in the backcourt, who could then run out the clock.

That's when Collins made one of the great plays in Olympic basketball history. Purposely hiding behind another player to elude Aleksandr Belov's field of view, Collins came out of nowhere, stole the ball, and made a mad dash for the opposing basket. Collins had plenty of room to pull up for a short jumper for the win, but he knew that if he drove to the basket, the worst he could do was get fouled and shoot two free throws. Collins was fouled so hard by Sakandelidze on the way to the hoop that when he flew into the stanchion, his head slid *under* it. Collins was knocked out for several seconds. The game clock showed three seconds remaining.

As the trainer rushed out to Collins and his teammates gathered around, Bach was mentally scanning the roster to choose a substitute to shoot two of the most pressure-packed free throws in basketball history. This wasn't to win a collegiate title or an NBA game, but rather to win an Olympic gold medal against a Cold War enemy. But there was only one person Iba trusted to shoot the two shots. He told Bach and Haskins, "If Doug can walk, he is going to shoot."

On the Soviet side, Sergei Belov was fuming. Aleksandr Belov's terrible decision to pass the ball away from the Soviet basket out toward the U.S. basket had not only resulted in the Collins steal but also had given the American guard a 30-foot head start toward the basket with only Sakandelidze able to get back to challenge him. It was the perfect example of what Iba had predicted would happen many times if the U.S. stuck to its plan: the Soviets would be too exhausted and too overcome by the occasion to win in the end. If Collins made his shots and the U.S. won, Iba would surely go down as one of the giants of U.S. basketball and cement a record likely never to be equalled—coaching three straight Olympic basketball teams to gold.

Collins made his first attempt, and the crowd exhaled in an explosion of noise. Then, just as an oddly mistimed buzzer sounded, Collins released his second shot. Swish. U.S.A. 50, Soviet Union 49. Bedlam reigned in the basketballhalle. After 39 minutes and 57 seconds, the Americans had their first lead of the game.

The Soviets inbounded the ball to Sergei Belov, but Collins forced the Soviet star to dribble a couple of precious seconds off the clock looking for an opening. "I'm guarding him and I'm standing back and turning him twice, and the game is basically over," Collins recalled. But with Belov 60 feet from his basket and the Soviet coaches and players spilling onto the court gesturing wildly, referee Renato Righetto of Brazil, generally known as an outstanding FIBA official and one of the few at the Olympic tournament whom most players and coaches acknowledged had been consistently good in Munich, blew his whistle to restore order with a single second remaining.

Soviet assistant coach Sergei Bashkin had left the designated bench area—which should have resulted in a technical foul—to assert that head coach Vladimir Kondrashin had called timeout between Collins's first and second free throws, and that the hand-held buzzer the coach used to signal timeouts had malfunctioned. Apparently, the mysterious buzzer that sounded before Collins released his second foul shot was the attempt by the timekeeper to recognize a Soviet timeout. According to the rules, however, a timeout could not be recognized once a player possesses the ball for his second free throw. Even though Righetto eventually ruled that the Soviet Union should not be awarded a timeout, the U.S.S.R. still got a huge break, as the clock had been stopped with Belov's dribbling and having no chance to score. Halting the game for no reason other than the chaos on the Soviet bench, with the U.S.S.R. about to run out of time, can be considered the game officials' **unprecedented ruling number one**.

Regardless of that mistake, common sense would dictate that only one second remained when play restarted. This is when R. William Jones, a legend in international basketball, took charge. The cofounder and then-president of FIBA, Jones strode down from his seat just above the scorer's table and held up three fingers, insisting that three seconds, not one, be put back on the clock. Righetto, after some confused discussion with the Bulgarian referee and the German scorekeepers with whom he didn't share a language, finally obliged. Under pressure from Jones, Righetto had essentially wiped out the previous play. This was **unprecedented ruling number two.** As Bill Wall, who at the time worked for the U.S. Olympic Basketball Committee, put it years later, "the entire life for those officials and everyone at the scorer's table was dependent on Dr. Jones, especially the Eastern Europeans. To come out from behind the Iron Curtain in those days was phenomenal, and if you ticked off Dr. Jones you never got out."

For the past 40 years, Americans have been questioning what right Jones had to influence the game that night. In some ways it's understandable why the British Jones felt entitled to do so. For four decades he had been the world's most well-known non-American basketball executive. A staunch advocate of international basketball, he teamed with Dr. Elmer Berry to create FIBA in 1932, and had been spreading the game's gospel ever since. Having organized all international basketball tournaments since 1936, including the Olympic Games, Jones determined the eligibility of every international team in both the Eastern and Western Hemispheres.

That Jones, as a non-American, proved the driving force behind basketball's becoming an Olympic sport is not widely recognized in the U.S., the sport's birthplace. But for all his vision, the man who invented basketball at Springfield College in Massachusetts, Canadian James Naismith, was never the international sports figure that Jones was. Whereas Naismith went on to study medicine and become the athletic director at the University of Kansas, Jones spearheaded the game's spread around the globe. As the first non-American inducted into the Naismith Memorial Basketball Hall of Fame, Jones had been a force for good. Nonetheless, he was known as the iron-fisted dictator of international basketball, and he later admitted he technically had no authority over on-court rulings.

Ever since the four-minute mark, Gifford had been alone in the booth; Russell had started to make his way down to the sidelines, and, hopefully, the U.S. locker room, for postgame interviews. Gifford acknowledged he was totally confused by the turn of events and had no idea why three seconds would be put back on the clock when, clearly, the game had been stopped with only one tick left. As Iba, Haskins and Bach continued to question the decision, Gifford correctly noted that what neither team could afford at that point was a technical foul.

After the Soviets inbounded the ball a second time, the horn sounded as Modestas Paulauskas' heave from more than half-court caromed harmlessly off the backboard, signaling an apparent American victory. After many fits and starts, this young American team had finally done it, and Iba had led his third United States team to a gold medal. It had all been worth it: the pressure-packed tryout at the Air Force Academy, the three-a-day practices at the spartan Pearl Harbor base, the barnstorming exhibition tour against NBA stars, the months of playing a style of basketball few of the players had been familiar with or even enjoyed at all. This band of college kids had beaten the crafty and physical Soviets, essentially a team of professionals who, on average, were almost eight years older than the Americans. "Wow, what a finish," Gifford exclaimed on the ABC broadcast. "This place has gone crazy." Dwight Jones recalled that it hit him hard that they had won the gold medal. "I was elated," he said. "The euphoria was everywhere." Even Henderson and McMillen, who didn't exactly see eye-to-eye on everything, were hugging. The long ordeal was over and the team could go home as Olympic gold medal winners.

For an American fan, it is painful to watch footage of the players' celebration, knowing what is coming. As officials start to speak to the Americans again, Gifford explained, "Again we are being told the scoreboard is not correct. Apparently they are going to reset the clock back at three seconds again." As the commotion at the scorer's table intensified, the Americans slowly stopped celebrating and strained to understand this new round of frantic negotiations between Jones, the scorekeepers, the officials, and the coaches. "They are telling them to come back on the court," an incredulous Gifford told viewers.

Jones, still standing over the scorer's table, insisted the clock had been reset incorrectly and hadn't actually shown three seconds remaining when play resumed. The timekeepers heeded his orders by restoring the three seconds once again—**unprecedented ruling number three**. "Everybody is jumping up and down, and then Jones comes out and says we have got to reset the clock because the scorer's table wasn't ready," said McMillen. "It would be like David Stern coming out in the middle of a Laker game and saying, 'I don't want the Lakers to win,' and so they reset the clock. That was the real travesty."

The American coaches knew, as did anyone who understood the game, that officials in that situation were supposed to keep their own count of the final seconds in their head—just as soccer referees do—on the slim chance of a scoreboard malfunction or other disturbance. At the scorer's table, Bach stood toe-to-toe with Jones and told him, "You can't put time back on the clock sir; only God can do it." Jones was unmoved. Iba, angrily confronting FIBA officials and the two referees, had to be restrained by his players.

Instead of playing on, Haskins wanted to pull the team off the floor. "Let's pack up the balls and get to the locker room," he said to Iba within earshot of several players. But according to Bach, R. William Jones told the coaches that if the Americans left the court not only would the team forfeit the gold medal, future U.S. teams could be barred from Olympic basketball competition. Iba told Bach and Haskins,"I don't want to lose this game later tonight sitting on my butt in the locker room."

Mike D'Antoni, who was one of the players cut from the 1972 team and who would go on to coach the Phoenix Suns and the New York Knicks, believes Iba did the right thing given the inconsistent refereeing that had been in evidence throughout the tournament and how things had gone topsy-turvy in the final game. "I think you play through it and you just hope that it works out for the best," D'Antoni said, "Obviously it went wrong,".

In retrospect, given the whole situation, it wasn't Iba's finest hour. First, keeping the team on the floor granted legitimacy to the decision to again place three seconds back on the clock. Second, in his heated exchanges with FIBA officials and the scorekeepers, Iba essentially forgot about putting the right players on the floor, leaving the same small team out there during all three last-second Soviet attempts to score. Tom Burleson, the seldom-used 7-foot-2 center, languished on the bench even though his giant wingspan could have eclipsed the view down court of Ivan Edeshko, the Soviet player taking the ball out of bounds. Burleson was in Iba's doghouse for a number of reasons, so even though he was begging the coaches to put him in for the final sequence, Burleson later explained, "they just told me to sit down and shut up." The team's best jumper and defensive player, Bobby Jones, was also stuck on the pine, doing his play-by-play for the concussed Jim Brewer. "I think Iba at the time was just out of it," Ratleff said, looking back. "All this stuff was going too fast, he wasn't thinking about it, and he was just trying to get the game over with."

As the inbounder of the ball, Edeshko was more quarterback than basketball player. The Soviets' plan was simple: throw a long pass to Aleksandr Belov under the basket 90 feet away and hope he can catch the ball and lay it in. Before halftime of two exhibition games against the Americans just a few months earlier, Edeshko had thrown two perfect length-of-the-court strikes for baskets. In Soviet league play, one of his last-second full-court passes had won a game the previous year for his team against Spartak Leningrad, a team coached by Soviet Olympic coach Kondrashin. So Kondrashin clearly knew what to do with Edeshko. It's unclear if anyone on the U.S. side was aware of the strength and accuracy of Edeshko's full-court passes, but Gifford presciently noted, "There is still time to go to their big man, Aleksandr Belov. They are going to try."

After he gave the ball to Edeshko, Artenik Arabadjian, the Bulgarian referee, gestured toward McMillen—who was assigned to cover the passer—and appeared to caution him not to break the plane by reaching over the end line. "What's he telling me? Is he telling me to get off the ball?" McMillen recalled. "I just didn't know."

McMillen was aware that under international rules a defender was allowed to get up on the inbounds passer as long as the passer had room behind him, and Edeshko had plenty of room. Yet McMillen moved back several feet, almost to the free throw line. There was also a Soviet player to his right whom McMillen saw and drifted toward, apparently hoping to cut off that safety-valve option. According to McMillen, the crazy events that had already occurred made him want to avoid getting a technical foul. "In that situation, you just don't want to make a mistake," McMillen said. "And our guys at the other end covering Belov just didn't want to foul. We became defensive." Bobby Knight, a disciple of Iba's who was never one to criticize the late coach, did disagree with the strategy of putting a defender on the pass in that situation, because then there was one less defender near the basket.

Edeshko wound up and whipped a high, long pass all the way down the court. Joyce, playing just a bit past half court toward the U.S. basket to pick up Sergei Belov in case the dangerous guard received the ball, sprinted to help the 6-7 Forbes, the sole American who was back with the 6-10 Aleksandr Belov. Rising between a catawampus Forbes and the onrushing Joyce, Belov caught the pass with his arms outstretched. Joyce jumped a little early and his momentum carried him well past Belov and out-of-bounds. Forbes lost his balance coming down and ended up flat on his back. Belov gave one small fake, perhaps thinking that a totally open lay-up was too good to be true, and laid the ball in off the backboard for the winning shot as time ran out. Moments earlier the goat for throwing the pass that was intercepted by Collins, Belov now became the hero. At 1:18 A.M. Munich time, the U.S. had lost its first Olympic basketball game, 51-50.

"Aleksandr Belov, between two American defenders," a stunned Gifford managed. "And this time it *is* over." Describing the American players and coaches as stunned would be an understatement, according to Collins, who, had the Americans won, would surely stand today as one of America's all-time Olympic heroes. "After we won, I remember running the length of the court and just jumping into Eddie Ratliff's arms," Collins said. "We were best friends; that was my guy. I always say it's like somebody taking you up to the top of the Sears Tower in Chicago and saying you're the champions and then pushing you off. You've won and then you're free-falling."

During halftime and other breaks in its Olympics broadcasts, ABC would often cut to Chris Schenkel, who was handling the in-studio duties and transitions to other sports. Schenkel was obviously struggling to find his footing when he said, "You know, we've covered a lot of basketball games over the years for ABC and I don't think there has ever been a basketball game that has me so totally confused as the ending of this one ... The Russians, almost in a sneak play, came back and they won, 51-50."

Iba, meanwhile, was shouting at the scorer's table to anyone within earshot. "I don't think it's possible to have that take place in three seconds," he said. "There's no damn way he can get that shot off in three seconds." An angry Bantom threw a towel out toward the center of the court. Forbes desperately kept crossing his arms back and forth to indicate the play was no good or occurred after the final buzzer had gone off. But according to the referees, there was no foul or violation on the final play, although contact did occur as Aleksandr Belov landed with the ball and Forbes was knocked off balance. After those protestations failed, Forbes was in tears and didn't care who saw him crying. Forty years later, he remains hauted by the final play. "I think about it every day of my life," Forbes said. "It's burdensome sometimes. You ask yourself maybe if I'd fronted him, maybe if I had bumped him a little harder instead of getting knocked down. I think every day of my life that I let the United States down."

Although no one blamed Forbes for Belov's outjumping him, several American players believe Belov would not have been able to knock Dwight Jones or Jim Brewer to the floor and get a free look at the basket. "If Dwight would have been in the game, if you push him and he's falling, you're going to fall too," Bantom said. "He never would have been standing there unaware and gotten pushed in the back and taken out of the play."

Envisioning a protest, Iba refused to sign the scorebook. While over the years many commentators have repeated that the Brazilian referee also did not sign the scorebook, in fact he did, even though he later said he considered the Americans the true winners of the game.

CHAPTER 27
Strange Bedfellows

Shakespeare wrote in *The Tempest* that "misery makes strange bedfellows." That might explain some of the strange bedfellows thrown together by fate in the aftermath of the game: Frank Gifford alone in a darkened arena with the Soviet players, Kevin Joyce sitting with ABC producers in a television control room.

After Belov's winning layup, the Soviet players didn't celebrate under the basket where he scored but instead at the opposite hoop, in front of the Soviet bench. Belov, arms aloft, sprinted all the way to the other side of the court to be enveloped by his teammates. The Soviet players were rolling around on the floor, hugging each other and the team's coaches and trainers, drinking from bottles of vodka that had appeared out of nowhere. From their point of view, as Sergei Belov would say many times throughout the years, justice had been done; they deserved to win because they had played the better game. "The win in the gold medal game in Munich was a gift from the heavens for all the hard work we had done," he once told an interviewer.

As the Soviets rejoiced, the men and women who were broadcasting the game hustled to alter what they thought would be—despite the cliff-hanger—the same old ending to the Olympic basketball script. Dennis Lewin, the ABC sports producer assigned to the telecast, had anticipated a U.S. victory even when the Americans were trailing in the second half. "You have to remember," Lewin said, "the Americans had won every game in the history of the Olympic basketball tournament. We were going over just to do their next win." It was Lewin who had sent Bill Russell down to the floor with about four minutes remaining to get the (presumably) winning interview with Hank Iba.

Russell's early departure from the booth was probably a good thing. Throughout the Olympics, he had displayed a penchant for directness that could have threatened ABC's ability to retain rights to the Olympics. At one point earlier in the night, after a strange officiating call from Arabadjian,

137

Russell asked rhetorically, "Well, what do you expect from a Bulgarian referee?"" There's no telling what Russell might have said during the chaos that marked the three chances the Soviets were given to score. "Bill was there on a lark," recalled Gifford. "He was there having fun. He was a little bored looking at guys trying to play his sport, but he was terrific."

As it turned out, Iba and the American players were in no mood to be interviewed by Russell or anyone else. For one thing, in a perfect metaphor to describe the end of the game, Iba's pocket had been picked during the confusion on the court; almost $400 had been stolen. For another, the American players stormed back to the locker room as Russell trailed, trying to get an interview. But Russell hadn't seen how the game had ended; he was making his way courtside and by the time he got there it was too late. "So Russell is down in the locker room without a monitor, and I was trying to explain to him in his ear what happened with the whole last sequence," Lewin said.

The scene in the locker room was chaotic. Some players were despondent; others gathered to form a plan. Players cried and screamed at what they considered a gross injustice. Iba, still visibly stunned, came in and said to the team in his low voice, "Well boys, let's suck it up and go out and get our medals." Joyce told him to get out of the locker room. The Games were over and it wasn't Iba's team anymore. The 63-game winning streak, the streak of seven straight gold medals, the apparent come-from-behind victory over a supremely talented and disciplined Soviet team—it all had been shattered in an instant. The players soon decided that if the protest that was sure to be filed did not result in reversing the outcome of the game, they would refuse to accept the silver medals.

Before a vote was taken, however, the studious McMillen raised questions about not taking the medals. "It's one of those things that you have to weigh, and I probably threw out some alternatives," McMillen remembered. Knowing there was likely to be a formal protest filed and sensing the players might be up to something, officials from USA Basketball, along with the coaches, came into the locker room and tried to get the players to commit to accepting their silver medals. But it was unanimous: the players said the only medals they would ever accept would be gold, and that if the protest failed they would boycott the medal ceremony. Kenny Davis, acting as the player representative, told the press about the players' decision. At the ceremony the next day, as the Soviet Union and Cuba teams accepted their gold and bronze medals, respectively, the public address announcer intoned, "The United States team refused to accept the silver medal—they believe they deserve the gold."

It was left to Iba to lodge the official protest that immediately prompted a FIBA appeal hearing in the dead of night. Iba also addressed questions at a packed postgame news conference, where he said, "I've never seen anything like this in all my years of basketball." Joyce told the gathered media that, "The whole world knows we won. Now we are sitting here left with nothing. It is a disgrace."

The control room, where Lewin was working, also was in an uproar. Knowing the U.S. would protest, which would affect the nuances of how ABC would present the gold medal game, Lewin nonetheless had to start editing the Olympic sports package for that evening's prime-time telecast. But people began knocking on the door. One of them was David Wolpert, a well-known filmmaker and television producer who had been commissioned by the IOC to make the official film of the Munich Games. Wolpert wanted to see the tape of the game, the angles of the last play, coverage of the scorer's table during the controversy, anything he could get his hands on. Lewin kicked him out. "There were so many people trying to fly in and out of the control room, and I'm trying to do a job," Lewin said. "The president of the United States could have come in that door and I wouldn't have cared. I had a job to do."

Soon enough, some of the American players started to come in to see replays of the final three seconds. Joyce and Collins asked to review the final sequence. At one point, Lewin, committed to staying on the story until the IOC announced something definitive related to the U.S. protest, left the control room and went into the darkened arena and sat with Gifford in the broadcast booth. There, sprawled out on the floor and on a mishmash of chairs on the sidelines, was the entire Soviet contingent: players still in their uniforms, coaches, trainers, assistants. They, too, were waiting to find out what would become of their gold medal victory. As 2 A.M. turned to 3 A.M., the American players started leaving in small groups. Burleson and McMillen went to a West German brew house. Joyce sought out his mother and Collins his fiancée (the two women had watched the game together). Lewin eventually went back to his room at the Sheraton Munich Hotel, and ABC broadcast the game and signed off without knowing the result of the protest.

Typically, FIBA's technical committee would first rule and then its Jury of Appeal would weigh in if a team was still dissatisfied that its case hadn't been understood. Given that the Olympics were ending the next day and the magnitude of the controversy, however, the hearings were held concurrently. The FIBA members on the Jury of Appeal hailed from Poland, Cuba, Puerto Rico, Italy and Hungary. The Munich Games already had experienced so many protests and incidents related to the athletic contests that the jury must have felt like a Brooklyn traffic court. Only after Egypt pulled out of the Olympics following the terrorist attack did the official from Hungary, Ferenc Hepp, take the place of the Egyptian member of the panel, Abdel Moneim Wahby. To the Americans, the makeup of the jury looked suspicious. Iba and Haskins actually flew back to the U.S. on the first flight available the next morning, sure what the result of the protest would be.

But the potential of a straight party line vote, in retrospect, was actually the least of the Americans' problems. Archived documents at the Olympic Museum make clear that the real issue at the hearing was that the jury was using Jones, as the head of FIBA, as its primary source on what happened during the sequence of events at the end of the game. But Jones never recounted his own unwarranted involvement in the game. In the minutes of the emergency IOC executive committee meeting from the early morning of September 10, just hours after the game, it's written that "Mr. William Jones, Secretary General of the Federation Internationale de Basketball Amateur assisted during this part of the meeting." In this emergency meeting, during which Jones was supposed to provide a blow-by-blow account of the confusion, he never even mentioned his participation as the major actor at the scorer's table. Not until more than a year later would he acknowledge his central role.

In his testimony during those wee hours, Jones glossed over the controversy surrounding the game and went straight to the issue of what was to be done about the U.S.'s refusal to accept the silver medals. "Mr. Jones continued that there was no rule in the Federation's rules concerning medals, but that the first three teams did qualify for the tournament in Montreal" at the 1976 Olympics, the archives report. "If the Americans lost their place, then they would have to re-qualify for Montreal…" Jones simply used a smokescreen to distract the committee from a real discussion of the events.

Brundage, perhaps sensing Jones was being evasive, explained that the crux of the protest was that the Americans "claimed that the first bell for time was the proper bell and they were the winners." Jones replied that by putting the ball back into play from the sideline with three seconds left, the referee had ruled, by definition, that the first buzzer that ended the game didn't count. Jones never volunteered the fact that he was the one who had ordered the referees to restore those fateful three seconds.

Another aspect of the protest that's been underreported concerns Jones's threat to Bach that if the U.S. pulled its players from the court and refused to play, the Americans would immediately forfeit the game and potentially be barred from future international competitions. According to the minutes from the executive session, several members of the IOC thought "the Americans should have protested immediately about playing the extra three seconds." In other words, if the Americans had refused to play after the game ended the first time—exactly what Haskins wanted them to do—their protest would have carried much more weight. But when they considered doing just that, Jones bullied the coaching staff into believing the game would be forfeited.

Eventually, at about 6 A.M., the Jury of Appeal said it would break and meet again at 11 A.M. to renew debate and vote on the U.S. protest. At about 1 P.M., it was announced that the panel—by a vote of 3-2 that went along party lines, with members from the communist nations of Cuba, Hungary and Poland in the majority—had rejected the U.S. appeal and the Soviet Union had indeed won the gold medal. The jury said it had looked at the last play from three different angles before rendering the decision. In traditional accounts of the protest lodged by the U.S., what seems most fishy to observers is the fact that the 3-2 vote ran down party lines; in other words, the U.S. never had a chance at a fair hearing. But in fact, Jones's misrepresentation of his own role marked the real scandal.

The U.S. players not only skipped the medal ceremony that was to be held in the 80,000-capacity Olympic Stadium but also left Munich

141

as quickly as they could. Tom Burleson was the only one who stayed for the closing ceremonies; he walked up to the stadium, looked around for a while, and never entered. As for the medal ceremony, after the U.S. team made clear it wasn't attending, the event was moved indoors, after the men's handball competition. Clearly the IOC wanted to "bury" the ceremony for fear of highlighting the fact that the Americans were not there and thereby generating more controversy.

In the press conference that followed FIBA's decision, members of the Western media, mostly U.S. reporters, crossed the sacred line from covering the event to participating in it by heckling the jury. According to Christopher Clark Elzey's dissertation on the Munich Games, sportswriters and broadcasters, some of whom had been up for 36 hours, got angrier and angrier with their questions. One scribe called Hepp "a goddamned liar." Another exclaimed, "We're not mentally retarded. Can we get an honest answer here?"

The most interesting development at the news conference was that West German scorekeeper Hans J. Tenschert either didn't get the memo from FIBA about how he was to act at the press conference, or else purposely went off the script. As Elzey noted, in the middle of the conference Tenschert tried to set the record straight, stating that, "When Mr. Righetto came to the table, he showed to us one second on the clock. There was no discussion between Righetto and any of us, only a hand signal … made by Mr. Jones." Tenschert also noted that Edward Bigot of France, FIBA's official scorer at the table, remained silent during the whole episode, blindly accepting Jones's assertion that three seconds be added. Referees Righetto of Brazil and Arabadjan of Bulgaria really didn't have a lot of choice if the official timekeeper agreed that more time should be added to the clock. Bigot's presumably frightened silence lends even more credibility to Bill Wall's observation that everyone at the scorer's table was basically concerned about his own livelihood if he didn't do exactly what Jones had ordered.

In the archives of the Munich Olympics are hundreds of letters written by Americans and fans of basketball around the world infuriated by the game's bizarre ending. "There is simply no doubt but that the American team was deprived of the win because of mistakes made in the administration of the event, which was further compounded by the refusal of the appeals board to recognize that which was obvious to all who could see: the third awarding of the ball to the Soviet team was wholly and completely unjustified under any reasonable interpretation of the events," wrote J. Riley, Ph.D., of Omaha, Nebraska. "The fact that the official scorekeepers attest to this conclusion is only additional proof of the unfairness of the 'official result.' I applaud the action of the American team in refusing to accept the silver medal and only wish that stronger action would be taken."

Then there was this letter, dated September 22, 1972, and addressed to Brundage from Jon Bliss of St. Louis, whose handwriting suggested a youngster of eight or nine years old: "The Olympic basketball game between the U.S.A. and Russia was unfair. The timekeeper said there were three seconds remaining, and the Russian player cannot call time-out after a free throw. When the Russian took the ball out his foot went over the line. What do you think about the basketball game?"

The acrimony over the game's ending wasn't limited to the fans. USOC President Clifford Buck went as far as to threaten that the United States would consider pulling out of future Olympic basketball tournaments organized by FIBA. The IOC said that Buck could file another formal written appeal, but in an indication of how seriously that protest would be addressed, the IOC announced it "wished to hear the protest of the United States Olympic Committee ... However, the next meeting concerning this matter will be in February in Lausanne, Switzerland." That was five months away.

The U.S. media, too, was outraged. Elzey quoted various U.S. publications that called the final three seconds of the game and its aftermath a "fiasco," a "travesty," even "Spassky's Revenge," a reference to American Bobby Fischer's victory over his Soviet opponent in the world chess championship. Even the normally balanced coverage of the Olympics in the *New York Times* dripped with sarcasm at the Soviets' "victory," citing two violations evident on film and the fact that, "The Soviet Union would have three chances to win in the final three seconds."

It goes without saying that the response in the Soviet Union was quite different, and the Soviet press didn't stop at basketball either. The Soviet media trumpeted the fact that its athletes ended the Munich Games with 50 gold medals, the most of any country. The U.S. won 33. In terms of total medals, the Soviets won 99 compared with the Americans' 93. The chairman

143

of the State Sports Committee went on Soviet television after the Games and declared that, "In 10 sports the Russians were the best and in 15 others, we were ahead of the Americans." According to the *Times,* the Soviet press agency Tass said the American protest had been "prompted by wounded pride." As far as the American team's decision not to attend the medals ceremony or accept the silver medals, Tass called it "simply unethical."

R. William Jones, who died in 1981, at one point admitted that although he might have overstepped his authority by conferring with the referees, he was only trying to pursue the fairest result. Jones said there was no way he thought the Soviets could score with three seconds left, having to traverse the entire court. His implication was that, in the end, it wasn't the fault of the scorekeepers, referees, or FIBA officials such as himself that the Soviets scored at the buzzer—it was no one's fault except that of the U.S. players and coaches who had fallen asleep, so to speak, on the last play.

But Jones's international pedigree and self-appointed role as a basketball missionary could have led him to be at least subconsciously biased in favor of the Soviets in the gold medal game, for a win by a country other than the United States promised to spark more worldwide interest in the sport and strip its veneer as one invented by and for Americans. Against those charges, it doesn't mean much to Bobby Knight that Jones is a fellow inductee into the Basketball Hall of Fame. "He didn't know a thing about basketball," Knight said. "There has never been an English team that could beat the Eskimos. It was political for a guy like Jones to be the president of international basketball."

```
⊠⊠
v130 l
v130
     u
   olympic basketball lead
   munich (ap)--russia was officially named olympic basket-
ball champion sunday after a 14-hour delay when a united states
protest of the gold medal game was thrown out.
   at a news conference, ferenc hepp of hungary, president of
the appeal jury of the international amateur basketball
federation (fiba) said the initial playing of the closing
three seconds had been ruled  not  valid.
   asked who had the authority to reset the clock at 0:03 and
give russia another crack at glory, hepp said referee
score's table.
   the united states had contended in its protest that
resetting of the clock was ordered by dr. william jones of
england, secretary general of fiba.
   they said jones should have been powerless while the game
was progress.
   hepp said a fiba official such as jones had the duty to act
in any doubtful situation and that the referee had accepted
the judgement.
   +we won, etc. 2nd graf olympic basketball 3 (v095l)
   fc1537gmt sept-10-72


⊠⊠'''''
v131 n l
```

CHAPTER 28

Twelve "Pieces of Silver"

Forty years after the game, the twelve "pieces of silver" as Gary Smith referred to them in a 1992 *Sports Illustrated* story, sit unclaimed in Lausanne, Switzerland. While the players' continued refusal to accept the silver medals is generally applauded by the basketball community and Americans with knowledge of the game, the team has come under severe criticism from some quarters. For example, Lefty Driesell, McMillen's former coach at Maryland, who attended the Munich Games, once said the only thing more bush-league than the Americans' losing to the Russians was their decision to reject the silver medals. (Driesell, in a more recent interview, couldn't recall ever saying this).

Another critic is Lewin, the ABC producer who worked the game. "I don't think they should have walked off without taking their medals," Lewin said. "I know nobody agrees with me on that. I think that if this happened the other way around, and the Soviets or East Germans had lost to us and didn't like the way it was called and didn't show up for the medals, we would have branded them as sore losers. I just thought it was wrong and to this day think it's wrong."

Lewin points out that, in his television career, he has covered numerous events in which bad calls were acknowledged to have changed the outcome. Yet in no other instance, he says, has the losing team refused to acknowledge the winners. He cites the famously blown call at first base in the sixth game of the 1985 World Series that led to the St. Louis Cardinals' losing the World Series to the Kansas City Royals. "It was my replays that showed they blew the call, and it changed the World Series," Lewin said. Speaking of the American basketball players at the Munich Games, he added, "I'm not saying they shouldn't have screamed that they got screwed, but I still would have taken the medal."

Mike Bantom speaks for many of the U.S. players, however, in saying: "You could make your argument for sportsmanship and that you are supposed to accept the outcome and congratulate the other guy. Hey, I would be the first guy to congratulate them. I'd be proud of winning the silver medal, if I won a silver medal. But we won a gold medal. We beat the Russians. I'm mad that we didn't beat them for 40 minutes and six extra seconds."

For his part, Iba never really got over the loss. When Iba returned from Munich that September, he talked about how the game had been handled so poorly, recalled Moe Iba, the coach's son. But after that, the controversy rarely came up; it was simply too painful to discuss. "In all those years after that was over, he never talked about it," Moe Iba said. "It was the biggest disappointment in his life to see the way the game ended for the players and the U.S."

No doubt the criticism of the U.S. team's playing style in Munich also stung, especially since, but for the final three-second debacle, Iba's vision of the final game—that the Americans would win if they held the Soviets to under 50 points—ended up being spot-on. Whether Iba willed that vision into fruition by insisting his players slow down the pace is another debate. Regardless, even the Soviet players would take jabs at Iba in the years to come. Sergei Belov, in a first-person article for an international basketball magazine in 1983, asserted: "Everyone who later analyzed this game was astounded by its low score; basketball had long grown unaccustomed to such low figures. However, the Americans were so constrained by rigid schemes that no opponent would have been able to change the character of the game … [T]his 'defense' was precisely the approach—and an unprofitable one at that—that U.S. coach Henry Iba took."

The Soviet players involved in the final play have their own issues to deal with. They hold a reunion every 10 years to mark the anniversary of their victory. Alexsandr Belov is long dead, having passed away from a rare heart tumor, known as cardiac sarcoma, in 1978 at the age of 26. But Ivan Edeshko told an American reporter at the World Basketball Championships several years ago that he was tired of answering questions about the final three seconds and that at a time of U.S. failure in Vietnam and the perception that America's power was on the wane, Iba and his team simply couldn't handle losing to the Soviets. To Edeshko and his teammates, their American opponents' failure to recognize the legitimacy of the Soviets' achievement still smarts.

In fact, not only do the U.S. players refuse to acknowledge that the Soviet team won, some are actively trying to redress what they still see as one of the greatest travesties in all of sports and certainly in all of Olympic history. At the Salt Lake City Winter Olympics in Salt Lake City, two Canadian pairs skaters finished second to a Russian duo. But a guilt-ridden French judge admitted that she had been "pressured" by officials in France's skating establishment to award a higher score to the Russians. The question for Jacques Rogge, the Belgian who led the IOC at the time, was whether the scandal cleared the IOC bar for intervening only on moral and ethical issues, as opposed to technical rules that the committee has always insisted must be left in the hands of the governing body of each sport.

When Rogge announced that duplicate gold medals would be awarded to the Canadian pair, Jamie Salé and David Pelletier, it shook figure skating's and other sports' international governing bodies, as so many of them were used to the IOC's doing nothing about such incidents for so long. After the IOC's ruling, Rogge was asked whether the decision could prompt pressure to reopen past Olympic controversies. Rogge responded that the only past cases that could be revisited were those in which there appeared to be "manipulation of the judgment," a standard that would seem to apply to the 1972 gold medal basketball game.

The whole ordeal at Salt Lake City was a revelation for Tom McMillen, particularly given that it took place on the 30th anniversary of the Munich Games. The former Maryland congressman became involved in an effort to convince the IOC to award duplicate gold medals to the American players using the Salt Lake City incident as a precedent. McMillen believed that a U.S. appeal, based on R. William Jones's inappropriate pressuring of the referees and timekeepers to put time back on the clock after the game had ended, could be viewed in a similar light to the figure skating scandal.

"I think we have a case," McMillen told the *Los Angeles Times* in 2002. "And I think it's worth exploring." McMillen received the go-ahead from each player to proceed, and then set to work on the appeal, sending a letter to Rogge asking that the game be officially revisited. In his letter to the IOC, McMillen cited "a blatant abuse of authority by Dr. Jones" as evidence of such manipulation. He also referred to the Americans' original protest, which was denied by the FIBA panel, 3-2, along communist and noncommunist lines. The IOC declined to revisit the game, however, prompting McMillen to try to arouse support on Capitol Hill, to little avail.

There was one person involved in the controversy who was not affiliated with either team yet seems to have thought a lot about that historic game over the years: Bulgarian referee Artenik Arabadjian. He ended up settling in New York City a couple of decades later. According to a person who once met him at Arabadjian's Queens home, the old ref would sit out in a lawn chair, trying to strike up conversations with passers-by about a basketball game that had happened years before. Very few people took Arabadjian up on his offer; mostly he would be alone with his memories, perhaps thinking of how things could have turned out differently on that long-ago September night.

Part VI

The Players and Coaches

The Players and the Coaches

JOHNNY BACH

Johnny Bach, one of two assistant coaches on the 1972 U.S. Olympic basketball team, has lived a full life, to say the least. Born in Brooklyn in 1924, the son of a merchant marine, he served in the Pacific in World War II; he lost a brother, a bomber pilot, to the war. Bach, a swingman at 6-foot-2, played college ball at Fordham and Brown. The Boston Celtics drafted him in 1948, and he had a brief professional career, cut short by injury.

He moved into the coaching ranks, landing the head job at Fordham to become one of the youngest college basketball coaches in the country. After 18 years at Fordham, Bach went to coach Penn State, reuniting on campus with Joe Paterno, an assistant football coach at the time, as well as head football coach Rip Engle and assistant Joe McMullen, all friends of Bach's from Brown.

In the mid-1980s, Bach moved on to the NBA, as head coach of the Golden State Warriors. He followed that up with five stints as an assistant coach in the league, including one with the Michael Jordan-era Chicago Bulls.

But few experiences in Bach's life stand out as much as what he and the entire U.S. team of players and coaches went through in preparing for *and competing in the '72 Summer Games. During the chaotic final moments of the gold medal game, when officials were resetting the clock for a second time, it was Bach who went to the scorer's table, sent by Head Coach Hank Iba, to try to find out what in the world was going on. Iba's other assistant coach, Don Haskins, remained with the players at the bench while Bach spoke to Renato William Jones, head of FIBA, the international amateur basketball federation, who had inexplicably stepped down from his seat in the stands.*

There was all kinds of talking going on—some in German, some in Russian. We had no translator. I couldn't tell what was being said. We had a Hungarian official, who spoke only French, and a Brazilian official, plus Renato, who spoke both languages. They had already talked before Iba sent me up. Dr. Jones came to me and said, "Put the United States team on the floor." I said, "You can't put time back on the clock, sir; only God can do it." He told me, "Tell Mr. Iba to put the United States back on the floor, or forfeit the gold medal."

Haskins wanted to take the guys off to the locker room. He said, "Let's go. Pack the balls and let's go home." Looking back now, we should have done it.

Iba could easily be interpreted as a gruff old man. He was a big, powerful man. People don't realize how big he was, and he had a reputation as being extremely strict. Actually, he didn't want the job. No one at age 68 should have that responsibility. No one would take it the third time. The committee took him because other people wouldn't take the job.

Mike Bantom wouldn't stand up straight during the national anthem. I remember Iba straightened that out. He said, "Line them up. We're going to stand straight and we're not going to go through this jiggling and moving and all that." Don't forget, this is a man that had coached 50 some-odd years, two prior Olympic gold-medal teams. Had guys like the Armed Forces guys, who knew how to stand, knew how to compete, knew how to not talk back.

During the Olympic tryouts at the Air Force Academy, there were staff sergeants at the doors, and I was glad, because it put handcuffs on people right away. The players were not allowed to walk across the quadrangle, no civilians were allowed to walk across it. That's beautiful history at the academy. It's only meant for Air Force people, and I wouldn't even think, as an old veteran, of walking across the grounds. Some of our players wanted to go through, and special police came right after them.

We followed a strict regimen. Early practice: hard drills. I mean hard, long drills because Coach Iba was a fundamentalist. It was hard-ass, let's see what they can do. One of his principles was that two good men can stop anything. Do you know what the drill was? Five-on-two.

Things were strict during the team's training at Pearl Harbor, too. You could eat what you wanted at the mess hall, but the rule in the military is: take all you want, but eat everything you take. So there were mess sergeants standing right at the garbage. You don't dump a tray with food on it.

We took the players over to look at the U.S.S. *Arizona*. I don't know if they appreciated Pearl Harbor and its history. They might have known something about it, but the (blood-stained) floor didn't mean as much to them as it did to me. I had lost my brother and I had gone through Pearl Harbor on my way to the war and I returned to Pearl Harbor. My ship came in. We saw the ships with, like, 400 caskets on deck. I mean, I've seen death and, you know, we didn't make fun of it. The players couldn't understand this ironclad discipline. Doug Collins said, "They don't have toilet seats." I said, "Doug, this is something that you have to recognize: They're training thousands of men, and they're not going to worry about a toilet seat."

I was a pilot and I took Kenny Davis for a flight around the islands in a little rented plane. We went to the other end of the island, turned around and came back. I said, "Let's fly the route that the Japanese flew on their way into Pearl Harbor." The plane's electrical system went out, and I lost my radio contact. When you fly and you have no communications, you're supposed to stay away from the field at a holding spot. But I hadn't done that; I kept hoping for the radio to come back on. So I left the holding spot on my own. I'm listening to traffic. I said, "Well, they just landed what they call a heavy, and they're not going to land two heavy planes one after the other. Maybe I can get in there." So I came in, approached the field and flew what they call down wind so that the tower can see me. I flew at 1,200 feet or something like that, and I'm waiting for them to give me the flags to come on in. I fly the last flag and I say, "God, I can't see anything, I don't hear any traffic coming in, I'm landing." So I went in and landed. Now I don't know which runway to taxi on. Certainly, I'm not taxiing with the heavies. So I headed toward what they call general aviation, and when I cut that engine, military personnel surrounded the aircraft because I'm an unlisted plane landing in Hawaii.

Once we got over to Germany, we went to a wreath ceremony at Dachau. Even the wildest cowboys we had on the team, the loosest young kids, were stricken by it.

The players deserve the gold medal. The coaches don't get one anyway. You know what Iba promised the coaches? He said, "If we win the gold medal, I have a friend in Oklahoma City who could make a medal for us." Apparently, he had done it for Iba after Tokyo and Mexico City. So I was looking forward to receiving that medal.

Courtesy of the US Olympic Committee

MIKE BANTOM

Each player went through his own remarkable journey during the Olympic tryouts, but none of them had quite the experience of Mike Bantom, now a senior vice president of player development for the NBA. Bantom was a good player, a strong forward from the streets of Philadelphia who impressed the coaches at the Air Force Academy with his rebounding and defense, and averaged more than 16 points per game to boot. Bantom was the most politically outspoken of the American players—in a way that Coach Hank Iba probably wished weren't the case.

I grew up in the projects, playing in the street. Did all kinds of little street games, but I never played any organized sports. I got into basketball kind of late, in ninth or tenth grade, just playing with friends but never organized. I didn't understand the game. I didn't practice the game. My high school coach was Speedy Morris. He kind of took a flyer on me. That was his first year of coaching. He said, "You're 6-5, maybe if I work with you for a year I can get something out of you." Turned out I had a real passion for the game once I started playing it. I really worked hard over the summer between my junior and senior year. By my senior year I was one of the best high school players in the country.

I made all-city my senior year and got a scholarship offer from St. Joseph's. My varsity coaches there were Jack McKinney and Jim Lynam. The Olympic tryouts took place between my junior and senior years. I asked McKinney, "How come these guys get to play on this team and I hear nothing about it?" Then, when the Olympic coaches invited everybody to the tryout in Colorado Springs, I was happy I got a chance to go out there and compete against the best players in the country. The first few days at the Air Force Academy, we spent just practicing, and at the end of practice we might scrimmage against the team that was playing on the other court. I remember that Mike D'Antoni was on my team.

I really didn't know who Hank Iba, Don Haskins and Johnny Bach were. I didn't know Iba was 68 years old at the time. Actually, he looked older than that. I was surprised that he could walk most days—he looked like he was about to fall over. There was always a large group of coaches who sat in the stands and watched and, I assume, evaluated us and probably had a voice or a vote in who made the team. I think they voted on talent, attitude and intelligence. They picked the guys they thought weren't going to be a problem and would be able to adapt to the coaches' system, guys like McMillen, Jones, me and Brewer, and not Marvin Barnes, Larry Kenon, guys like that. But ultimately we all fell in line and we bought into what we were supposed to do.

We broke after camp, went back home, then met back somewhere and went to Hawaii to train. That's when a lot of us wanted to quit. UCLA guys didn't come try out. The whole time people told us how tough the Russians were going to be, how these guys were going to knock our blocks off and they were going to be this and they were going to be that. But what we found out in game number one against Czechoslovakia was that these guys couldn't play and that we were going to kick their butt. They couldn't run and they couldn't handle our defense.

There was almost no security in the Olympic Village in Munich. Their idea of security was a bunch of college students wearing blue uniforms. I actually dated one of the security guards. We went in and out of the Village all the time; all you had to do was show your badge and you walked through. There wasn't any security out where the public walked. The kidnapping of the Israeli athletes took place right across the courtyard from where we were staying, in an identical building to ours. When we woke up that morning, there were guys standing on the terrace over there with guns. We woke up every morning and went to the trainer's room to get taped. Somebody would be on table, somebody would be sitting on a chair, somebody would be leaning out on the terrace waiting for their turn on the table, and when we walked in that morning, they said: "Somebody got shot last night. There's police over there right now, and they're guarding the area." The terrorists were still inside holding the hostages.

Olympic officials' intent that day was to get us out of the Village, and so they rounded us up and took us out to practice. Usually, we would go back in the afternoon to the Village and rest and then go back and have another practice later on in the day. But this day they didn't bring us back; they made us stay in the gym. I remember we sat around on the floor. We took naps just lying around, asking, "Why can't we go back?" We didn't know the seriousness of what had happened. They didn't tell us. I think it was purposeful. We realized that up until that point there was nothing to prevent anybody from coming into the Village and doing whatever they wanted.

You always had the sense that you were away from home. Our first reaction was just go home, it's not that important. It was just scary the way the German police handled everything. It was bad enough that these guys came in and kidnapped these folks and were going to kill them, but then the German solution seemed to be to shoot everybody. It's like, well, this is crazy. We need to get the hell out of here. After that, our bus got stopped by security guards every time we came into the Village. They got on the bus and checked everybody's card, but the horse was out of the barn already.

Courtesy of the US Olympic Committee

JIM BREWER

Seven months after that chaotic night on a basketball court in Munich, Jim Brewer got selected by the Cleveland Cavaliers as the No. 2 overall pick (behind his Olympic teammate Doug Collins) in the 1973 NBA draft. Brewer, the power forward from the University of Minnesota who could dominate both ends of the floor, was about to begin the next chapter of his life. But he couldn't completely move on. The sudden, unexplainable turn of events in the final three seconds of the deciding game against the Soviets that robbed the U.S. team of gold medals continued to claw at him. It would for years.

"I was bitter for a long, long time," Brewer, who went on to have a nine-year NBA career that culminated with a stint on the Los Angeles Lakers of Magic Johnson and Kareem Abdul Jabbar, told Sports Illustrated in a 20th anniversary story about the Munich Games. "I remember one day, about three or four years after those Olympics. I was looking for my passport in some cardboard boxes in the basement because I had to leave the country. And I came upon some pictures of the guys on that team, and some letters from that time, and I just started crying. I sat there for a while, alone in the basement, and cried. I finally let it go that day." Brewer was an assistant coach in the NBA for many years and is now a motivational speaker.

I grew up in Melrose Park, Illinois, outside Chicago. I don't think my father or mother played any sports. My father was a crane operator for Reynolds Metals for 35 years. My mother stayed at home most of the time but also worked as a domestic helper. One day when I was coming home from school in the sixth grade, I saw a guy with a basketball uniform and he said that I should come and try out for the team. I had been playing on the playground, so I went and I tried

157

out. I was 5-foot-5 at the beginning of the year. By my freshman year in high school, I was 6-6. I was measured at 6-9 at the University of Minnesota.

The one thing that really got me during the Olympic experience was the training. We did it three times a day. I think they looked at how we could work together, the temperament of the guys, because you had some pretty strong personalities in Coach Haskins, Iba and Bach. They were no nonsense kind of people. They were trying to pick this cross-section, the guys who would buy into the team concept.

Pearl Harbor was a dump. It was really a militaristic setting. We ate in the Navy commissary and you would go there and you would eat, like, a hamburger and french fries. They had you isolated. It wasn't quite as extreme as being in jail because everything in jail is restricted. You were able to get around freely on the base, but you had to go along with all the rules. One day we went to a hangar and they have all these shot-up airplanes. Iba wanted us to see them because at that time the U.S. was flying secret missions over to Vietnam. All of the fighter planes had an insignia on them. This was the death squad.

I saw a lot of security at the Olympic Village before the massacre. What I recall is that Germans at that time were very big on uniforms. Some police-men would have on their police uniforms. On the outside of the building you had guys who were army. They were in gray uniforms. They would drive us to different places and they were stationed at certain areas within and outside the area. Still, I knew some guys were slipping in and out of the Village. One of the reasons why people got in was because they were doing some new construction that they hadn't finished, so it was like a work area. They weren't going to finish it and there were people coming over that fence.

We could all see the terrorists. When you went into the cafeteria, there was one guy out there with the headdress and the rifle. You couldn't miss him. He stood out on that balcony most of the day. I was asleep when the kidnap-pings took place. Kevin Joyce was up listening to the Armed Forces Radio. I said, "What's going on?" He told me the whole story, but he listened to the radio in order to substantiate whatever it was. At that point, they knew the terror-ists had broken in and were holding hostages. Olympic officials weren't letting people know, but they were looking for Mark Spitz to get him out of the Village. Anybody of Jewish descent, they were taking out of the Village. And we're like, Well, why are they doing that? Later we found out that the Palestinians had shot these guys and were holding other hostages.

At that point, we were all in a state of shock, including the coaches and most of the other Olympians. We didn't know how to react. So we were kind of in a holding pattern, thinking, What's going to happen next? I had mixed emo-tions about whether the Games should have been cancelled. I said if they had to cancel them, I could understand. I admired Howard Cossell and how he spoke up about it and came to us to say, "You guys shouldn't play."

Jim Brewer at an Olympic parade in Maywood, Illinois. Also pictured riding on the back of the vehicle, current Boston Celtics coach Doc Rivers (Courtesy of Jim Brewer).

Courtesy of the US Olympic Committee

TOM BURLESON

Of all the players on the U.S. team, Tom Burleson, a 7-foot-2 future NBA center from rural North Carolina, today director of planning and inspections in Avery County, North Carolina, had the closest brush with the Palestinian kidnappers and Israeli hostages. The day after the Israeli athletes were taken captive at gunpoint, the American players were told to stay in their rooms until they went to practice and that, after practice, they could tour Munich. Burleson chose the latter, taking in the sights with his fiancée. When he returned to the Olympic Village later that afternoon, he found a crowd of about 500 people at a security checkpoint. To sidestep the crush of people, he decided to enter through the garage of the team's dorm. After he slipped out the back, a dozen German soldiers approached him, speaking in German. He couldn't understand them, but said he was going back to his room. He kept walking until another German soldier approached. This one spoke English.

"Young man, you are in the wrong place," the soldier said to Burleson. "They are getting ready to bring the hostages out, and you are right in the middle of it. So stand there and face the wall with your hands on the wall."

"I was right inside the garage door," Burleson explains. "I can still see the blemishes in the concrete in that wall. He put his gun to my back. The leader of the terrorists stepped around the corner and I see him out of the corner of my eye. The German soldier takes the gun from my back to my head and says, "Face the wall and don't move." I am now frozen against the wall and praying for my life when I should have been praying for the hostages' lives. As they brought the hostages behind me, I couldn't see them, but I could hear the emotion of the Israeli athletes, their crying and feet shuffling. I still wake up with nightmares of the emotion of those athletes."

I grew up in a farming family in North Carolina, mainly working my uncle's farm. He raised beef cattle. We had about 65 acres, including beans and hay. My father, who was a former Green Beret, saw my athletic potential when I was in about the third grade. He would get me up in the morning and we would run three miles, come back and do jumping jacks, sit-ups, pull-ups, sprints, and push-ups. That lasted until I was a senior in high school. All the hard work paid off. I was the top high school player in the country my senior year, according to Street & Smith magazine, and I was recruited by everybody except UCLA. My agricultural background helped me select North Carolina State.

I was an all-around player: second in assists at North Carolina State and the leading scorer and rebounder in the ACC. But I was on a 16-10 team. Coach Norm Sloan called me into his office and told me I had been selected for the Olympic tryouts. When he explained it to me and I saw all the other players who were selected, I was totally elated. The minute I got my letter, I started training. When I showed up to camp, I was ready for the elevation. I loved to run, I had very good legs and could jump. I really took Bill Walton's place. When he didn't play, it opened things up for me.

During the tryout camp, everyone was calling me a liar because I said, "I have a friend back at North Carolina State who's a freshman and he's better than any player here." Everyone said: "You're crazy. You're nuts. You're just off the wall." But years later Doug Collins came up to me when we were playing an NBA game in Philadelphia and said, "The guy you were talking about at the Olympic camp was David Thompson, wasn't it?" I said yes, and he said, "You were right."

Everyone on the team thought I was a hillbilly. Race was a big issue at that time. Tom McMillen warmed up to me when he came in for Swen Nater. I hung out with Bobby Jones, Kenny Davis and Doug Collins. Our whole team bonded in Hawaii. They put us in a barracks that was partially destroyed during the bombing of Pearl Harbor. We didn't even have mosquito nets and we were getting eaten up. Sailors there who saw us said we had it worse than they did in boot camp.

At the Olympics, we blew out everyone except the Russians. We had a tremendous team put together, but we should have played full-court pressing, playing to our strengths instead of the slow-down game. We knew the Russian players shot 1,500 shots per day. They took their three best shots and shot them 500 times a day. So when you don't pressure them on defense and they are shooting 17- to 20-foot shots, that is in the bank for them. Playing slow with them was a slow, methodical death.

But I have accepted the loss and I would take the silver medal today because as a Christian I have to forgive and forget. If the team votes to accept the

161

silver medal, I will accept it. I was only a pawn in this mess. I was 19 years old, a utility player. My role was very insignificant. God worked through me and I was the last athlete that the Israelis had contact with, about 45 minutes before they died. That whole scenario gives me nightmares. I didn't share that story with many people during the Olympics because I was afraid of being sent home.

The night of the kidnappings, we actually heard the gunfire. We were two buildings away and I said, "Someone is shooting off firecrackers celebrating." Kevin Joyce said, "I'm from New York, that's gunfire." I said, "You have to be kidding me." We went back to sleep and woke up that morning and the Olympic Village was under siege. The coaches told us to stay close to our rooms and go eat. I went to the mess hall and they had pictures of the hostages. I realized I had sat with these people one or two days before.

Courtesy of the US Olympic Committee

DOUG COLLINS

By any measure, Doug Collins, today the coach of the Philadelphia 76ers, has fared spectacularly well in life, but his experience at the Munich Games may be the most tragic of any of the 12 players' on the U.S. team. If his two free throws sealed the victory, Collins would be known today not only as a superb NBA player, a Hall of Fame broadcaster and the one-time coach of Michael Jordan's Chicago Bulls but also as one of the country's great Olympic heroes. Collins's free throws would have kept the Americans' gold-medal streak alive until the 1988 Games in Barcelona, where another loss to the Soviets prompted the outrage that led to the formation of the Dream Team of professionals that included Magic Johnson and Larry Bird in 1992.

Years later, Collins, then broadcasting for TNT, interviewed Sergei Belov about the Russian national team that his old rival was coaching. It was their first meeting since the gold medal game nearly two decades earlier. Collins asked him questions through an interpreter for about 15 minutes before thanking Belov and turning to leave. That's when Collins heard the Russian address him in perfect English: "I wish your son well this year." Collins's son, Chris, was a member of the Duke University basketball team. Belov was being sarcastic. Collins was livid that Belov, even 20 years after the historic game, seemed to enjoy tweaking him.

But perhaps in a case of cosmic justice, Collins is the only member of the 1972 team who actually possesses an Olympic gold medal for basketball. Chris Collins, today an associate head coach with Mike Krzyzewski at Duke, served as an assistant to "Coach K" on the 2008 U.S. Olympic team that took the gold in Beijing. When the elder Collins was inducted into the Basketball Hall of Fame, Chris took his own medal and placed it around his father's neck, saying it was his until he received the gold medal he truly deserved. Says Collins: "I

163

want to give my son his medal back."

Being at Illinois State, I was sort of an unknown. I had to beg to get an invitation to the Olympic trials. I don't know if a lot of people realized how the process worked, but they sent out 67 or 68 invitations for guys to come to Colorado Springs to try out for the team. When I got my invitation, I was on cloud nine. My coach called me into his office and told me. It was in the spring of my junior year, right after our season had finished. To prepare for the tryouts, I spent three to four hours in the gym every day, running. We were going to Colorado Springs and I knew it was going to be in the altitude, so I was going to be in the best condition possible. I just prepared myself to go in and do the best that I could do. After a few days at the tryouts, I felt like I could play with anybody, even the cream of the crop, the players from much bigger schools. The light went on for me that I could do it.

If you looked at it historically, they said they would take a guy from the Armed Forces, a guy from the AAU, someone from junior college. You would lie there in bed and just want to get some sleep because you were burning so much emotional energy. They divided us into teams. You had seven days of practice where you were with your team, and then you played seven games. We played every team one time. We practiced in Block Arena. It was an open-air arena with a tin roof. We'd go in there in the morning, practice for a couple of hours, and then go lie down. Sometimes we practiced three times a day. You would try to steal any kind of sleep you could. We stayed in the barracks, and they would play a different movie every night, or we'd go to the bowling alley and grab a bite of food. You marked the day off the calendar and woke up and did the same thing over again. It was hard. We went to Pearl Harbor to train and stayed in barracks. The 1992 Dream Team went to Monte Carlo and stayed in $1,000-a-night suites. Make no bones about it, the tryout was one of the toughest three weeks I've ever spent. The barracks were open-air. We were told it was where they brought the bodies when Pearl Harbor was bombed. There was blood on the floor that they varnished over as a memorial to the sailors. Coach Johnny Bach was an incredible military guy and he would tell us stories about what sacred ground this was.

I can still remember when we learned who had made the team. We went to a breakfast. You're sitting there with 58 other guys who have all tried out and the coaches are going to announce the 12 guys who have made the squad. You're sitting there and your heart is jumping out of your chest. They announced the names in alphabetical order. I think it was: Jim Brewer, Burleson, Bantom then myself. Bantom has said he doesn't think they picked the best players but rather the smartest. Maybe the coaches' thinking was that they only had a short window to try to put this together, so they were trying to assemble the group they thought would come together the quickest.

We practiced at high speed, but we were very deliberate in terms of our shots. The ball had to be passed a certain number of times. We played with an incredible amount of intensity on the defensive end. The total emphasis was on defending. If you didn't defend, you weren't going to play. I didn't care what style we played. I was so thrilled to be on the team. I've never been one to question what the coach is doing. I was always taught the coach knows what's right. But I think at the end of the day, in Coach Iba's mind, his strength was teaching defense and I think he felt that that's the way you win. One of the first times we got together for practice after we had made the team, he wrote the number 50 on the blackboard. "We're going to play the Russians in the gold medal game and they're not going to score 50 points against us," Iba said, "and we're going to win." Well, had my free throws stood up we would have beaten them, 50 to 49. That's how driven he was defensively with our group.

I'll never forget how I found out about the terrorist attack in Munich. Eddie Ratleff and I got up that morning to go to breakfast in the Village and as we were walking along I looked up and saw the terrorists on the terrace with their machine guns, their hand grenades, their masks. We had no idea what was going on. We turned around and went right back to the dorm. Just then, the helicopters came in and whisked away the terrorists and hostages. Later, when we heard about the shootouts, we were obviously all devastated. It was hard because there was that part of us that said, you know, we have come this close and we'd love to be able to finish the Games; and then there was that part of us that wanted to show respect for these athletes who had lost their lives. I think the healing process started when we went to the memorial service and got a chance to pay our respects.

When my fiancée, Kathy, wanted to come into the Village with me, she would just flash my photo ID and they would sort of just glance at it and she would go in. I had my USA warm-ups on, so I just walked in with her. After the shootings, there was a ton of security, a military presence. It put everything into perspective. You think of the Olympics as everybody getting together and, for a two-week period, putting all our differences aside and having this competition to bring out the best in each other. Then, at that point, the reality set in. This to me was really a rude awakening that the cold war was going on and that terrorism and all this stuff was real in our world.

Courtesy of the US Olympic Committee

KENNY DAVIS

Of all the members of the 1972 U.S. Olympic basketball team, no one has gone to greater lengths than Kenny Davis to ensure they never accept silver medals for having lost—officially, at least—the decisive game to the Soviets. It was Davis, as the team captain, who led the players' steadfast refusal to be so honored at the awards ceremony of the Munich Summer Games. Since then, he's dug in even further, albeit more personally, establishing a clause in his will forbidding his wife or children from accepting his medal after his death. "Anything can happen after you die, so I figured, I'll put it where they can't get it; I'll spell it out in my will," Davis, a principled son of a Kentucky farmer once told Gary Smith of Sports Illustrated. "We won the gold. The silver isn't mine. That's not sour grapes. It's the truth."

Davis, a motivational speaker and long-time sales representative of the Converse shoe company, has said the outcome of the gold medal game upset him more than it did any of his teammates. He was the oldest player on the team (two months shy of his 24th birthday), and the only one without prospects of playing professional basketball. "I came from a little NAIA school, Georgetown College in Kentucky, and I wasn't going on to pro ball like the others," he told Smith. "The Olympics was the culmination of all I'd worked for. To have the gold in my hand and watch it slip away. ... I went back to my room and cried alone that night." Still, a sense of perspective is never far from his mind. "Every time I get to feeling sorry for myself, I think of the Israeli kids who were killed at those Games."

I went to Wayne County High School in Monticello, Kentucky. My senior year was the first time we won the District championship in basketball in 40-something years. I led the state in scoring as a senior, averaging 32 points a game, but I did not make the East-West All-Star team nor the Kentucky-Indiana All-Star team. I was third team all-state. I graduated in 1966 and signed with Western Kentucky University. I went straight from high school to Western Kentucky. Stayed there about 10 weeks and a situation came up with my scholarship that wasn't justified or rectified, so I left there and went to Georgetown College in Kentucky. I sat out for the remainder of that year and went on to play four years at Georgetown (setting a school record of 3,003 career points). I graduated in 1971.

The Olympics wasn't the first time I played overseas. In 1969, I went with a group of collegiate all-stars, sponsored by the State Department, to Morocco, Turkey, Belgium and France, and then we ended up behind the Iron Curtain in Poland and Czechoslovakia. In 1970, I was on the World University Games team in Colombia. I think that was a better team than the 1972 Olympic team. We had Paul Westphal, Luke Witte from Ohio State, Jim Chones from Marquette, and Bob McAdoo, plus George McGinnis, Jim McDaniels and Jimmy Clemmons. Still, we ended up losing to Russia in the finals. That Russian team was a little bit different from the Olympic team we played, but not much. The next year, I tried out for and made the Pan-Am team. We lost in the first round.

I was playing for the Marathon Oil team in the AAU when I was invited to the Olympic tryout. I got a letter from the U.S. Olympic organization saying I was one of the representatives from the AAU who had an invitation to try out. For the longest time the AAU had been in charge of the players who went to the Olympics. It's probably true that in 1972 Olympic officials had to have someone from the AAU on the 12-man roster. When I went to the tryout, I was in the best shape I had ever been in my life. I told myself that if I didn't make it because I was out of shape, I would regret that the rest of my life. There were some very good players who didn't make the team, including Marvin Barnes, Larry Kenon and Kermit Washington. In the case of Barnes and Washington, their attitudes cost them, would be my guess. I think Coach Iba was behind that, because he knew that we were going to have to spend almost 30 days in Hawaii together and he didn't want anybody who would cause trouble there and when we went overseas. We all got along. There wasn't any fussing and fighting, and so I'm assuming from that standpoint, the coaches did a good job picking that team. The players or whoever can nitpick all they want, but I don't think it's fair to criticize Coach Iba.

When we were at training camp in Pearl Harbor, we stayed in the barracks where the sailors were. It was strange—there were flies and mosquitoes and that kind of stuff. We spent 26 days there. After we arrived, Swen Nater quit the team. I think he would have made quite a bit of difference. According to Bobby Knight, Bill Walton would have had a free pass to the Olympics had he chosen to play. If Walton had taken them up on that, I think the rest of us would have resented it with what we had to go through to get to that point, especially all the training at Pearl Harbor.

All during the day of the kidnapping of the Israelis, there was nothing we could do. They brought German troops in and completely surrounded the Olympic Village. Nobody was able to leave or get in. So we just sat there, trying to watch it and see what was happening. You could see the guy with that ski mask on. I had gone to breakfast that morning and walked pretty close by that building and saw some commotion. But I didn't know what was happening. I think we heard the news from some German officials. Then we came back and we stayed in our rooms, milling around, because they didn't suspend the games until about 1 or 2 in the afternoon. We could watch the live coverage of the kidnapping on television, but it was in German.

I think if you had taken a poll of whether the guys on our team wanted to carry on with the Games after that, the results would have been we'd go home. But looking back on it, I think Avery Brundage was right. He stopped the Games temporarily, everyone paid their respects, but then you have to recover. If he had canceled the games, it would have given the terrorists exactly what they wanted. I think that fear set in. We didn't know what was going to happen. It turned the Olympic Village from a festive atmosphere to something like a military camp. We had people stationed at our door; we had guards on our floor. At that point, we were just trying to find a way to get back home and get out of there.

THE WHITE HOUSE

WASHINGTON

September 12, 1972

Dear Mr. Davis:

I know how disappointed you must
be after the final game last
Saturday, but you may be certain
your fellow citizens still think
of you as champions. You played
with outstanding skill, and on
behalf of all Americans, I want
to congratulate you for a splendid
come-from-behind performance.

With my best wishes,

Sincerely,

Richard Nixon

Trustee shall have the power to pay out all or part of the principal if he judges it prudent for my child's welfare.

ARTICLE VI

I nominate and appoint Marvin Renfro Trustee of the trust created in Article V and direct that he may qualify and serve without surety on his Bond. Except as limited in Article V, the Trustee shall have all power allowed by law, including the power to sell real property without court approval.

ARTICLE VII

If either of my children are minors at my death, my spouse shall be the guardian of my children. If my spouse is unable to be guardian, I appoint Marvin Renfro guardian of my minor child/children.

ARTICLE VIII

I nominate and appoint my spouse, Rita Davis, executrix and direct that she may qualify and serve without surety on her bond. I nominate and appoint Ralph Davis and Marvin Renfro substitute co-executors and direct that they may qualify and serve without surety on their bond. I give my substitute co-executors the power to sell real property without further court order and to make distribution in kind.

ARTICLE IX

I devise and bequeath at my death that my wife Rita, and children, Jill and Bryan, and their descendants never accept a silver medal from the 1972 Olympic Games in Munich, West Germany.

In witness and affirmation, I have signed this last will in the presence of the persons witnessing it at my request this _____18 3_____ day of _JuLy_ 1991.

Kenneth B Davis
Kenneth B. Davis

Courtesy of the US Olympic Committee

JIM FORBES

Needless to say, the sudden, shocking turn of events that snatched victory from the United States in the 1972 gold medal game still weighs on every member of the team. But Jim Forbes has a singular burden to bear. Forbes, a slender forward from the University of Texas El Paso who had made the squad as an alternate, faced the challenge of guarding Soviet star Aleksandr Belov on the final play. When Belov caught a desperate length-of-the-court heave from teammate Ivan Edeshko, Forbes was sent falling to the floor. Belov quickly gathered himself and laid in the (official, at least) winning basket.

"I can't help but go there," Forbes says of the memory. "All these years later, you ask yourself, maybe if I'd have fronted him, maybe if I had bumped him a little bit harder instead of getting knocked down ... I think about it every day of my life."

Forbes agrees with the widely held perception that Belov initiated the contact between them. "He gave me a shove," says Forbes, adding that he was reluctant to closely guard the Soviet player for fear of being whistled for a foul.

Adding to his misfortune, Forbes suffered a knee injury while coming down from a lay-up during training back home in Texas a few weeks after the Olympics. He underwent surgery, and although he managed to play out his career at UTEP, he never was fully healthy again. Chosen in the fourth round of the 1974 NBA draft, he tried unsuccessfully to break into the professional game. "Chicago drafted me and I went to their camp for a couple of years, " says Forbes, now a longtime high school basketball coach and teacher in El Paso. "The second year I was basically done. The knee was gone.

Trying out for the Olympic team was one of the toughest things I've ever done. You had to compete every day against someone who wanted your spot. You are in a self-contained atmosphere and you've got 59 guys all shooting for a spot. Everybody's trying to do the best they can to impress not only the coaches that they had but the selection committee as well.

There had to have been some thinking among U.S. officials that they didn't want to see a display of black power in Munich like the demonstration on the medal stand in Mexico City. As a black athlete, I was never directly told any of that, but I'm sure that in the entire Olympic process it had to have crossed some of those committee members' minds. I have the utmost respect for John Carlos and Tommie Smith, to be honest with you. What they did took an awful lot of courage. They paid a price for it, but they felt it was worth it. They knew the consequences of what was going to happen. Whether you agreed or disagreed with them, they took a stand.

My first response to the Israeli hostage crisis was that the Games should have been canceled. Then when authorities said they had been released, everybody was happy. You felt for the two who had been killed, but the loss of life was limited. Then a little while later all of them had been killed, and that has a profound effect on you. My initial response was, call this stuff off and go home. I later changed my mind.

To this day, I have a lot of friends who totally disagree with me. They say we should have cancelled the Games out of respect for the athletes, but I say no, you *continue* the Games because of those athletes.

I think the emotional toll from the murders could have played a factor in our performance. I'm not saying that with other teams, it didn't affect them as well. But you've got to remember: the United States is a strong ally of Israel.

Another factor we had to deal with was the 11:45 p.m. starting time for the gold medal game, a decision that was made so the game could be shown on prime time in the United States. I thought it was bad because you wake up in the morning and eat breakfast. You go eat lunch. Scouting report review. Eat dinner. Another scouting report. And then you finally play the game at 11:45 at night. You're talking a little bit late.

In the locker room before the game, things felt a little different because of the tension. There are no more games left to play, this is it. You don't get a do-over. This is the gold medal game. You don't get to go back and play a preliminary round or play a semifinal game. This is the game that everyone came to see. There is a lot of pressure—pressure on both teams, the coaching staff, the players and everybody. Plus, there's a lot of pent-up, nervous anticipation because you've been up all day.

There have been other disappointments, but if I had to rank all the disap-

172

pointments in my life, the 1972 gold medal game would rank at the top.

The entire experience taught me a couple of important things. Sports is often not fair. Life as we know it is not fair. We look at the terrorist act that took place and took the lives of those individuals who were competing just like we were and it taught me to be humble. Be humble, be happy with what you do have and don't worry about what you don't have.

Courtesy of the US Olympic Committee

TOM HENDERSON

As a child of 1960s New York City who was raised by a single mother and once skipped school for 40 days after a dispute with a teacher, Tom Henderson is nothing if not independent-minded. When Henderson, today a licensed administrator for residential treatment in Houston, looks back on the 1972 U.S. Olympic basketball team, he's convinced that without the constraints placed on them by their coaches he and his teammates would have trounced the Soviets in the gold medal game. Head Coach Hank Iba, who at age 68 seemed out of touch with the athleticism of his young charges, insisted they play a slow, defensive style of basketball. The Soviets won the controversial final game by a score of 51-50.

"If you think about it, we had young deers," says Henderson, a fleet-footed guard who went on to be a first-round draft pick of the Atlanta Hawks and to win the NBA finals in 1978 on a Washington Bullets team that included future Hall of Famers Elvin Hayes and Wes Unseld. "I was in shape enough to play two games. I mean, I could run really long. We should have ran them back to Russia." Speaking of the talented scorers he had the good fortune of passing the ball to, Henderson says, "I had Doug Collins. I had Dwight Jones, who played at 6-10 and played hard down low if you just give him the ball. We should have scored hundreds of points—we had scorers. All they had to do was throw the ball out and leave us alone."

I was born in Newbury, South Carolina, but I grew up in New York City. My father died when I was 12. My mom was a single parent and there were eight of us. My mom never saw me play basketball until I played on the Olympic team. I had been playing for six years, but she was a single parent trying to make sure we had food on the table, so she didn't have any time. I got into basketball when I was 13 and just kept playing and playing and got better and better.

My senior year at DeWitt Clinton High School, I averaged 20 points per game. I played in four all-star games in New York and won four MVPs. I went to college at the University of Hawaii.

After I made the team at the tryouts in Colorado Springs, I called my mom and I went home for a week. I went to get a haircut. I'm at the barbershop where I've been going for about 10 years, and this barber says, "This kid Henderson made the Olympic team." He says, "This kid Henderson is a hell of a player. You know, he made the Olympic team." He didn't have a clue. So I tell him my name is Thomas Henderson. It floored him, because he's telling all his buddies that he knows me and all that. He ain't got a clue. He don't know me from Adam.

There was a lot of anti-American sentiment at the Olympics. I went to the track events with Rod Milburn (who won the gold medal in the 110-meter hurdles). I tell you, it was anti-U.S., because they gave the track players different schedules, so they missed a couple of heats. It just seemed like everybody was cold. It was just a cold feeling. When you went to the Olympic Village or whatnot, nobody really talked to you.

I didn't really notice much security in the Village before the kidnappings. There were security guys walking around with blue uniforms, but it wasn't heavy security. The day after the hostage taking, there was a whole buzzing around the place, so we turned a TV on and watched it. I think the coaches probably called us and told us what we needed to do. I felt it was a terrible thing, but I was never really afraid because the terrorists didn't want any black guys. They got the people they wanted. They didn't want us. They'd been fighting for hundreds of years. They talk about being religious and all. I don't get that part. I felt kind of empty for a minute. You felt high for a minute because you figured, okay, we got through that and everything is good. And then you come to find out that no, the Israelis didn't make it.

I thought the Games should have been canceled, but in retrospect, you let them win if you cancel. The terrorists succeeded in doing what they were trying to do. You continue on and you rise above it and not let them win. That's my feeling about it.

In the final game, Sergei Belov was kicking my butt. He was tough. He was a grown man. You know, that's his job. That's what they do. We didn't scout them at all. We didn't watch them. In hindsight, we should have watched their games—see what he does, see what makes him feel uncomfortable. That's how you get into his head.

The biggest problem, though, was that Coach Iba had us playing too slow and cautious. That stuff wasn't working. We had to go to another plan. That's when Kevin Joyce stood up in the huddle, told the coaches to put him in and

175

said we need to run and press. Now we're playing our game again. We were freewheeling. We're not setting up, taking our time. We're coming at them. We are forcing the issue. If we had done that from the first ten minutes of the game, there would have been no contest. We would have run them back to Russia. We only ran the last five or six minutes. By that point, we were going to press. What Iba said didn't matter—that wasn't working. We were doing our own playing.

After everything that happened at the end of the final game, I wasn't going to accept a silver medal. We all agreed in the locker room: We're not taking the silver medals. It's in my will. I think I was the first one to tell my kids that if I die, don't take no silver damn medal.

Courtesy of the US Olympic Committee

BOBBY JONES

Bobby Jones, the former University of North Carolina and Philadelphia 76ers star, doesn't do angry, doesn't do bitterness, doesn't do what-might-have-been. Jones, one of the great defensive stoppers in basketball history, was sitting on the bench when Aleksandr Belov laid the ball in, uncontested, at the buzzer to clinch the Soviets' controversial victory. These days, Jones spends much of his time doing Christian outreach—and thus is in the business of forgiveness—but he is still in no mood to completely forgive and forget. Every few years he gets letters from the International Olympic Committee addressed to "Bobby Jones, 1972 silver medalist" and asking if he will reconsider accepting his medal. Jones throws the letters in the garbage. "It took some guts for us to say, 'We are not going to accept the silver medals,'" Jones says. "We knew there would be consequences and it would look like we are bitter, but I didn't concern myself with that. I was angry that this rip-off had taken place."

The anger Jones still harbors makes his overall philosophy on that historic game all the more incredible. The year after the Munich Olympics, Jones played against some of the same Soviets again, this time during a Soviet tour of the United States. Some of the Soviet players stayed in the same hotels as the Americans, and Jones struck up conversations with them, not so much about the game as about their daily lives. It dawned on him that the Soviets' Olympic victory had been a salvation for the team's players, a lifelong ticket to a decent apartment, a new car every few years, an income to put food on the table for their children. For the Americans, the loss was just that—a defeat in a basketball game. "A lot of things came into focus for me then," Jones says. "That game made their lives. They said if they hadn't done that, they'd be with the Russian Army in Siberia."

I was a high school All-American in Charlotte, North Carolina, and got recruited nationally, ending up at the University of North Carolina, where I played for Dean Smith and graduated in 1974. When the Olympic tryouts were being planned, I was unaware of them. Coach Smith either came by or called me; I can't remember which. He said, "Bobby, did you know that the Olympic tryouts are taking place in a week or two in Colorado Springs?" And I said no, I didn't. He told me George Karl, one of my teammates, was going. "He said, 'A lot of guys have declined their invitation. Bill Walton's protesting the war and Marvin Barnes might not be there because he may be in trouble with the law or something.'" So there were a couple of vacancies.

At the tryouts, they divided all 59 of us into teams. I wasn't a nationally known player by any means. Dean Smith and Bobby Knight, who was one of the coaches at the tryout, obviously had different styles. But they were both looking for somebody who was going to do what they asked him to do, and that was one of the few strengths I had. If a coach told me to do something, I was going to do it. I never thought about it, and so I think Coach Knight liked that and he liked the fact that I played defense. Before the very last game of the tryouts, Coach Knight came into the locker room and said: "Now listen,"—and he was brutally honest—"there's two guys on this seven-man team right here that have a chance of making it." He said I was one of them, and that my teammates needed to get me the ball. I went on to have a pretty good game and ended up making the Olympic team. The next morning was a Sunday. They had a big banquet at which they announced the team. Everyone was just sitting out, all 59 guys. The coaches said, "We need the following men," and they named the team and you stood up. I was stunned that I had made it. I ran back to the dorm to call my dad to tell him.

The team they chose was a pretty fast team, although that was not the style of play we used. We were separated for a while and we met up at Travis Air Force Base in San Francisco, practiced for a few days and then we took a military transfer to Hawaii to the submarine base there. We had three practices a day in this pavilion on the base, open-air but sunk below ground. When we first got there we stayed in a condemned building. I don't want to call it a slum, but there were rats running around.

In the Olympic Village, we stayed in the middle of three buildings and the Israelis were in one of the outside buildings. Right when the attack happened, I heard what I thought were fireworks that turned out to be gunfire. I thought it was just someone shooting off firecrackers, so I went back to sleep. I woke up the next morning to an armed camp. Underneath our building where they had all the transportation, there were military vehicles lined up. The scariest thing when I look back on it is that when they took the hostages out in the helicopters, the other Olympic athletes were in this common area and the terrorists were right there with machine guns and could have taken out a couple of hundred people. I saw a few of the terrorists from a distance. I think the coaches or managers called to let us know what was going on and when to come to practice. I was really saddened by what happened. I was sure they would cancel the Olympics. That was my first awareness of terrorism. I had no desire to play basketball. It was a tragedy. We were at practice a lot and I don't remember watching the events on T.V. I'm not a guy to show emotion when someone dies, but in this situation it was different because they were fellow athletes. I think it affected us all a great deal.

As far as the games went, we were never overconfident or took anyone lightly. I give the coaches credit for that. The Russians were very physical and mature. The gold medal game was intense. It was the most physical of all the games we had played. The refs seemed to let more go, like in an NBA playoff game. I remember taking a charge and then coming out. I don't remember going back in. Jim Brewer had a concussion and I sat with him. He didn't know where he was. His condition worried me more than the game.

Courtesy of the US Olympic Committee

DWIGHT JONES

On a team of highly talented U.S. players, Dwight Jones, a 6-foot-10-inch center/forward from the University of Houston, stood out. He could run the floor with anyone. Shoot. Defend. Box out. Over the nine games the Americans played in the Olympics, Jones tied for the team lead in scoring (with Tom Henderson, at 9.2 points per game) and led the team in rebounding (5.7 per game).

So it was no small loss to the United States when the referees ejected Jones in the second half of the gold medal game for getting into a scuffle with a Soviet player over a loose ball. That player, Mishako Korkia, hadn't played much in the Olympics up until that point, leading the American players to conclude that the Soviet coaches had inserted him into the game with the express purpose of baiting Jones. "I know he was sent in there to hit me," says Jones, who went on to a 10-year career in the NBA and now manages a car dealership in Houston. "I got a rebound and he hit me after that."

Jones recalls being struck from behind on the play and then turning around and raising a fist, for which he was promptly thrown out of the game—just as the Americans were launching the heroic comeback that would culminate with Doug Collins's two free throws to give them a 50-49 lead with three seconds to play. "I didn't touch him," Jones says of Korkia. "Somebody grabbed my arm, so it wasn't touching another player."

I can still remember when the coaches announced in Colorado Springs who had made the team. We were sitting in a big cafeteria and they were calling out the guys that were going to Hawaii. They would call out different names and I was in the back of the room. They said, "Starting center, Dwight Jones." I guess they named the alternates first and then the regular team. I don't know

180

how many alternates they named, but when they called my name I took off running. I didn't know my name was going to be called out, because there had been so many good players at the tryouts. I just hoped and prayed that I made it. I thought I was in contention because of the way I had played. I didn't back down to anyone.

I didn't think a lot about the style of play that Coach Hank Iba called for. I just know how I played—up-tempo, let's go, let's get out. I had no idea what kind of ball they played in the Olympics, what style, the international style or anything like that. I was just there to play. I wasn't dissecting who was there, who wasn't there or, is this going to be good for me? Just give me the basketball and I'm going to play. That's all I thought about.

When we got to the Olympic Village, I didn't pay any attention to how strict the security was there. I just know that we snuck out one time. Coming back, we saw they had closed the gate for getting in, and we climbed the fence. After the kidnappings, you could see the terrorists walking across the balconies. We were told to stay in our rooms, stay down until this stuff finishes and see what happens. They told us to get under the bed, the chairs or whatever; don't go near the windows. They kept a lot of the news from us until later. When we heard that the Israelis had been killed, we felt sorry for them. It was kind of frightening and threatening at the same time. We felt sorry for them, but we felt relieved that the terrorists weren't coming after us, too. I don't know whether the Games should have been canceled at that point. Stuff was so political at the time. It was one of the most political Olympics of all time.

I know the gold medal game was moved to 11:45 at night (so it could be shown in prime time in the United States), but I don't think it had any effect on us. As young as we were, I don't think time mattered to us because it wasn't our country anyway. We went through 50 million time zones trying to just play basketball. To me, I don't think it mattered.

If we had won the gold medal—and been awarded it as we deserved—we would have been just another U.S. team that won an Olympic gold medal. I guess our being denied the victory and our refusal to accept the silver medal made more people see me as a basketball player, but I don't think it changed my life. I haven't heard any negative talk about it. Even when we started playing basketball again, people didn't call us losers or silver medalists or any of that stuff.

It really wasn't difficult for us to agree not to accept the silver medals. We were used to winning and we came together as a group, as a team, as one. We all made the decision real quick. We didn't like the fact that we were cheated. We just said, "We're not taking them." We watched the medal ceremony—with the empty podium—on T.V.

I know that one of the Soviet players said on the HBO special that we should go over to Russia as a team so we can all sit around and talk about the game, have a couple of drinks, and be awarded the silver medals. Let them come over here and bring the gold medals.

Courtesy of the US Olympic Committee

KEVIN JOYCE

Kevin Joyce was a Wall Street trader for many years, and Wall Street traders are known to hurl verbal barbs at one another when things get dull on the trading floor. "Yeah, they stick it to me pretty good," Joyce once told an interviewer. A common gibe: "There goes the first guy who ever lost an Olympic gold medal in basketball."

Actually, had the final game not ended so controversially, Joyce would have been considered a hero. If his teammate Doug Collins provided what should have been the winning points on a pair of free throws, it was Joyce who made those free throws possible. It was he who finally stood up in a team huddle and said that Coach Hank Iba's slow-tempo style of play wasn't working—they needed a change. Once play resumed, the Americans mounted their historic comeback. All these years later, Joyce says, regarding Iba: "I think the game at that time had probably passed him by. He just thought, this is how you win Olympic basketball games, that nobody else knows how to win Olympic basketball games." The tense relationships between the players and Iba—who was nearly half a century older than his charges—would play out over the course of the Olympics.

The tryout for the Olympic team was war. It was probably one of the toughest things I've ever done because back then it added so much to your professional draft status, being an Olympian. Still, I always had the confidence I was going to make the team. In fact, I had a very good camp.

After the tryout, we all went home for a week before having to report to San Francisco, where we took off for training camp in Hawaii. I was almost sent home from Hawaii when I got a spasm in my back and had to sit out one practice. I'd had spasms before and I knew they would go away in, like, four days. But Iba told me, "You have two days, or you're out of here." I just went out and wore a brace around my back. After Hawaii, we went to Washington, D.C., where there was a big reception for us the night before we left for Germany, on chartered flights.

During the opening ceremonies in Munich, the weather was really hot. I remember standing in the infield, all of the athletes lined up by country. As soon as the doves were released, they pooped on everybody. That first week was a lot of fun, with all the other athletes and trading pins and things like that. The Olympic Village was great. Your parents and your families could come in and hang out. There was a disco in there. It was basically a city for us. The restaurant was open all the time. But once the attacks came, it was closed off. There were tanks at the gate. Nobody could come in. There was 24 hours that my mother had no idea what was going on or where I was.

We were under strict rules from then on. We weren't allowed to talk to a reporter without a coach being present. There were 20,000 police officers on the scene, but they were not in uniform. They patrolled the outside of the Village, checking security. I was sick the night of the kidnapping. I got up early that morning and heard what sounded like gunshots, but the Village was built over a parking lot and the old cars back then would backfire, so I didn't think anything of it. We did not know right away who was murdered. I don't think anybody knew what was happening inside the building. Once the massacre happened, we were gone. They took us to the Air Force base as a team.

I remember walking out after the semifinal game and knowing the gold medal would be decided the next day. I'm not angry, but as far as I'm concerned they gave us the wrong medal. I'm certainly not angry at the Russian players. I think all of a sudden politics got involved and somebody who wasn't supposed to be involved came down from the stands and started running the game. That shouldn't have happened. The refs lost control. They were putting time back on the clock.

We still had three seconds to make sure we were set up to go guard everybody, so the game wasn't over yet. But as far as I was concerned we won it, and then the buzzer sounds and we celebrate. Suddenly, there's people coming out and talking and some people you can't understand. They're trying to push people back, and Coach Iba is out there calling everybody back over, and you don't know what's going on. I saw somebody who wasn't involved in the game at the scorer's table talking to the timekeepers and the scorers. I was totally confused.

Then all of a sudden they put us out there and they turn the clock on and throw the ball in again. And then I think it's over again. After that, I'm basically pissed off at what's happening and how it went. The game ended and we celebrated and now they're doing this. I'm trying to just do what I'm told out there. You're talking about 20-year-old kids. We're just going through with what we're supposed to do. We couldn't, as players, make any arguments. We couldn't say anything. The refs didn't understand what we were saying. I don't think any of the refs spoke English. It was just more confusion.

Things started happening really quickly when they put the other three seconds on the clock. We just had to make sure somebody was guarding the ball. I was at half court because Sergei Belov was in the game and I knew that if he got the ball and took one step over half court, he could possibly make a shot. So I wasn't letting him alone. Aleksandr Belov was down below, and we had Jim Forbes on him. Everybody was playing man-to-man defense. There wasn't much talk about it—everybody knew who they had to guard. Well, I see the ball going long, so I start running to the baseline and try to get up in there. I pass Belov when he catches it. I'm standing out of bounds underneath the basket when he puts it in because I was running and trying to intercept the pass. I just flew right past him.

I was fairly vocal in the locker room afterward, but I wasn't the only one. At that point, we didn't know what the outcome was, but we knew the game was being protested. I'm not sure when we all decided that we wouldn't accept the silver medals. It had to be a players' decision—the coaches don't get medals, just the players. We knew we had to stand up for what we thought was right. As I recall, it was a unanimous decision. We weren't making a political statement whatsoever. There was no politics whatsoever in what we were trying to say. We weren't trying to say anything except, "It's the wrong medal."

Personally, I felt relieved when the Olympics were over. It had been a long run—tryouts, the training in Hawaii, three-a-days, stuff like that. I had to get back; I was already late for school. I was going to go home for a few days to spend time with my family and then head back to school at South Carolina. At the time, I wasn't thinking much about everything that had happened those last days in Munich. I thought we had made the decision we made and that was it.

Courtesy of the US Olympic Committee

BOBBY KNIGHT

Bobby Knight seldom played the role of supporting actor in the many dramas that defined his tempestuous coaching career. But he did just that in the saga of the 1972 U.S. Olympic Basketball Team, serving as one of a number of coaches asked to help out at the tryouts held at the Air Force Academy. Knight was 31 years old at the time. He had just completed his first season as coach at Indiana, where he would stay for 39 years, win three NCAA championships and burnish an image as one of the game's biggest personalities.

His secondary role with the '72 Olympic team notwithstanding, Knight has strong opinions about all that befell them. To this day, he's unsparing in his criticism of Bill Walton, then the top college basketball player in the nation, for turning down the chance to represent his country at the Summer Games in Munich, and of Swen Nater, Walton's teammate at UCLA, who quit the Olympic team during training camp in Hawaii.

Knight also remains a staunch supporter of Head Coach Hank Iba, a basketball legend whom many suggested was too out of touch with the up-tempo modern game by 1972 to effectively steer the team. One of those critics was Lefty Drisell, the coach at Maryland, who attended the '72 Olympics in support of his star player, Tom McMillen. "I thought it was really unfair," Knight says of the criticism. "There isn't a guy since 1940 that's coached basketball anywhere in the world that doesn't do something that Henry Iba initiated. Not one coach ever in the last 70 years—and most of them don't know where it came from.

The first time I met Iba was at a sports banquet in Akron, Ohio, where I was on a recruiting visit. He came up and I felt somebody's hand on my shoulder. Henry Iba was one of the most modest people I've ever met in my life.

I turned around and it was Coach Iba. And before I could say anything, he said, "Son, my name's Henry Iba." And I just laughed. I didn't know how else to respond. I laughed and I said, "Coach, I've known who you are since I first started playing basketball."

One day while I was coaching my squad in a practice game during the tryouts, an official called a technical foul on me. I'm saying, "Goddamn it. Let these kids play! We want to see who the hell can play." You know, "Stick that whistle up your butt!" or something. So he gives me a technical foul. So the next day, I wear a referee shirt and bring a whistle to coach. The next morning after that, I see Iba at breakfast. He's eating a bowl of cereal. As I approach him, he never looks up. He just goes, "I don't want to see that Goddamn referee shirt today."

The Air Force Academy was the perfect place to hold the tryouts, because you're 10 miles from Colorado Springs. I had the trials in Bloomington when I coached the Pan-American Games and then the Olympic Games. I had the guys staying in the (Indiana Memorial) Union to keep track of what the hell was going on. I mean, you can't let these kids on their own.

We played the Russians during that period when I was at Indiana. Probably five different times. And they were far and away the best team in the world. Then when I coached the Olympic team in 1984, there were four teams that could play besides us: Spain, Yugoslavia, Russia and Canada.

I missed the 1972 gold medal game on TV. But I remember listening to the radio when Collins was shooting the (go-ahead) free throw. It had to be a rebroadcast. And he made it, and I can remember telling whoever I was with, "Goddamn it, we won it! We won it!" And then all the commotion happened. I've been asked, 'Would you have taken the team out on the floor?' I don't think I would have. Not unless someone over me told me we had to go out on the floor.

The final play of the game, when the Russians scored, was a joke. First of all, the guy steps inbounds on the pass. He has not released the ball and he has crossed the line. Secondly, the guy that catches the ball shoves Forbes out of the way. And thirdly, he walked with the ball going to the bucket. So the officials should be castigated for what happened because there are three definite violations. If you know even a little bit about the game, you see the violation, you see the foul, you see the next violation. Blatant.

You can't blame Iba for the loss. His guys threw the ball away. They played poorly on defense. They took bad shots. Are those turnovers his fault? Are those bad shots his fault? No, these guys didn't play well.

If it had been up to me, I would have told Walton, "All right, they've given you a dispensation. You don't have to come to the trials. Once we bring the team together to start to work for the Olympics, then you'll have to be there." I don't

have any use for Walton, and he knows it. I just don't care for the guy at all because he was not incapacitated. He just didn't want to go. Nater, too. He came up
to me to say hello as I was doing a game with Brent Musburger in Seattle, and it
was all I could do to be polite.

Courtesy of the US Olympic Committee

TOM McMILLEN

Tom McMillen holds a unique perch in the game of basketball. As a high school senior he graced the cover of **Sports Illustrated** *as the top schoolboy player in the country. Along with Bill Bradley, he is one of only two NBA players who have ever been Rhodes Scholars. He is also the only NBA player ever to have run for Congress during his basketball career. McMillen began raising money for his campaign for Maryland's Fourth Congressional District seat during his final season, with the Washington Bullets. He won the election and went on to serve three terms in the House of Representatives. Today, McMillen is the CEO of an information services company. Yet for all of his accomplishments, McMillen still can't quite explain why he made the fateful decision to give Ivan Edeshko all that room in the waning seconds of the 1972 gold medal game to throw a length-of-the-court pass to Aleksandr Belov to set up the controversial winning basket.*

After all these years, it doesn't eat at me. If you put it in historical perspective, this was really the Cold War being played out in Munich, West Germany, at midnight September 10, 1972. That's really what it was. I had met President Nixon. I was on his Commission. I really didn't fully understand all the manifestations of the cold war and how it could be right smack in the middle of sports. But it was so important for the Soviets to show some kind of superiority to their system because they are fighting against the U.S., which is superior economically, probably superior militarily, and they had to keep some kind of hope alive for their people. That's why this was so important for them.

Although I was an All-American from the University of Maryland and had a strong tryout in Colorado Springs (averaging 15.1 points and 7.6 rebounds per game), I made the Olympic team only as an alternate. For some reason, I wasn't picked, but Swen Nater of UCLA was. I went home and was pretty disappointed. After Nater quit, Lefty Driesell, my coach at Maryland, told me I had to go to the training camp in Hawaii. It was the right thing to do, he said. Since Nater quit the team, I gained my spot.

In the Olympic Village in Munich, we were staying within a couple-minute walk of the Israelis. I remember watching the kidnapping on T.V. as Jim McKay was broadcasting live. There were crowds around and the terrorists were wearing black ski masks. We played our final game after the attacks. There were a lot of policemen. They were wearing sweatsuits. It was very surreal seeing these policemen with automatic weapons running through the Village in sweatsuits. We were concerned there might be other attacks. People were talking about the possibility of other attacks even while that one was going on. Olympic officials considered canceling the Games. I had mixed views because it was a pretty significant event to occur in the Olympic Village. I know our assistant coach Johnny Bach and I talked on the way to practice about whether the Games should go on. September 5 was when the Israelis were killed, and the next day we placed a wreath on Building 31, where they had stayed. I remember I went over to that ceremony, but it was tough. That was on a Wednesday, and Thursday was the semifinal game against Italy. Saturday night was the finals. We had woken up on Tuesday to this massacre of the Israelis—I've never gone from so high to so low in my life. In retrospect, I think it would have been a mistake to cancel the Games because it would have played into the hands of the terrorists. It would have been a terrible precedent to cancel the Olympics. Avery Brundage, president of the IOC, was right on that one.

We knew right from the beginning of the final game that it was going to be hard-fought. The Russians were tough. They were strong, fast and mature. Some of them were 10 years older than us and it was like playing an NBA team in a lot of respects. We knew we had ourselves a game. Fortunately, we started to play better in the second half. The first half we didn't play that well. The free throws Doug Collins made were two of the toughest free throws you could put an athlete through. Here's a guy in the Olympics with the U.S.'s whole legacy on the line—and he hits those shots. You can hear that when you go through the tape and look at it. The whole dispute was, were the Russians trying to call a timeout? My understanding is that they were trying to call a timeout before he took the second free throw, and you cannot do that. Actually, it was the assistant coach of Russia who left the bench and should have received a technical foul for being out of the coaching box. Then the horn sounds when Collins is shooting the second free throw, which is the scorers' trying to indicate the Russians asked for a timeout.

I remember there was a picture in a magazine and we were jumping around and I was very excited. That was after the second inbounds play, and we thought we had won the game. The first one was sort of confusing and maybe there was some legitimacy to it. So we're going to set up and the Russians do not score and that was when chaos broke out because we thought we had won the game. Everybody's jumping up and down, and then R. William Jones says we have to set the clock back another three seconds because the scorer's table wasn't ready. It would be like David Stern coming out in the middle of a Laker game and saying, "I don't want the Lakers to win," and so they reset the clock. That was the real travesty—and I was on the ball. I remember the Bulgarian referee, who didn't speak English, he's pointing at me like I'm supposed to get off the line. I'm not sure what he is saying, but I know that I don't want to end up getting a technical foul, given the way this thing is going and that they are going to find a way to screw the U.S. It was clear something was going on here where they were going to keep playing the game until the Russians won.

I was on the ball and they were pointing at me, but the Bulgarian referee denies telling me to back off. But if you look at his hands, you can see he's doing something. In international rules, if there is enough room in the back, you don't have to do that. But I wasn't going to take a chance of getting a technical foul. I mean, it's like you're trying to make an instantaneous decision as to what is right and what is wrong here, but, you know, who knows? Maybe he wasn't telling me that. How would you know?

I'm sure there were some questions from people asking me why did I step back. I explained to them that, given the craziness of the game even if I was on the ball, the guy could have thrown it past me. He had enough room behind him, so the question is, Belov caught the ball and scored and Joyce and Forbes didn't want to foul him, as that was their concern. So they weren't going to foul and kind of got out of the way when he caught it. Everybody was trying just to play it out and not make an error, which is sort of what I was playing out. So I think there was a little bit of that defensive posture going on.

It was pretty traumatic coming back to the U.S. after all we'd been through with the final game and the dispute over the medals. I had to get back to school. I remember I had classes that already had started, and here we are into September. I was a chemistry major; I had a tough curriculum. A lot of people wanted me to come speak also. There was a real demand to talk about this game.

Courtesy of the US Olympic Committee

ED RATLEFF

Ed Ratleff, an All-American swingman from Long Beach State, had a brief career with the Houston Rockets, after which he coached the women's basketball team at his alma mater. To this day, Ratleff, who now works in the insurance industry, believes more than any other player on the 1972 U.S. Olympic team that they beat themselves in the gold medal game. He cites not only the deliberate style of play instilled by Head Coach Hank Iba but also Dwight Jones's ejection midway through the second half, when the star big man got tangled up with an inferior Soviet player. "Dwight Jones should have known better," Ratleff says. "You play on in the game and hope you get him back. If you retaliate and you're in front of an audience in the Olympics, you're putting yourself in trouble because you're out in the open."

Ratleff's assertion that Jones got suckered into retaliating gibes with an anecdote told by teammate Mike Bantom. A few years after the Olympics, while Bantom was playing in Italy, some of the Italian players marveled to him about how surprised they were that the Americans had fallen for a trick like that. Trying to instigate an incident with the opposing team's best player happens all the time in international basketball, they said.

Ratleff is also of the belief that Iba, in addition to being out of touch with his team, played into the Soviets' hands with his slow-down offense. Ratleff even suggests that the athletic young Americans might have done better if they didn't have any coaches at all. "We had guys that could run and shoot," he says, "and I think we would have run teams out of the gym."

I got drafted by the Pittsburgh Pirates out of high school. We won the state championship in baseball and basketball my senior year, at Columbus East High School in Ohio, and I'd played baseball my whole life. But I also excelled

192

at basketball: I was All-American and in my senior year they asked me to go to the Dapper Dan game, the national high school all-star game. Our state all-star game was in Marion, Ohio. My senior year I played in that, too, scoring 30 points and winning MVP. Instead of playing professional baseball, I went on to Long Beach State in California and played basketball there. I was a two-time All-American and the sixth pick over all in the 1973 NBA draft. I also graduated in 1973.

The Olympic tryouts in Colorado Springs were very intense. We were practicing three times a day. Some guys might have left and gone home. I'm not sure. But it was tough. We were at practice all the time, then you played, and, believe it or not, you didn't get enough to eat—even though there was a lot of food there—because you're too tired to eat. You also didn't sleep very well. I think they picked the 12 guys that were going to stay out of trouble. I think what happens is if you think you're going to have problems with a guy, you don't take him.

At training camp in Honolulu, guys were getting mad because we're in Hawaii and we should go to the beach, but no, we're at camp. It was very tough because it was hot and humid. To practice three times a day, I don't think any one of us liked it. We had cots to sleep on and there were some rats running around. But I grew up in a tough area, so any rats wouldn't bother me. I think one day they finally let us have some time off in Pearl Harbor to go to the beach and the town.

When we got to Munich, they put us up on the second floor of one of the buildings in the Olympic Village. You could come and go, and you didn't think anything was going to happen. You're at a young age and we're all together. It wasn't like anybody was going to come into the Village to get you. Little did we know.

I never saw the terrorists. We heard all the commotion in the Village when we got up that morning. I think we still went to practice, and the coaches told us what had happened. As they were talking about it and going over it, we watched a little bit of the events unfold on TV. I wasn't afraid at all. You know what? First of all, it's not that you're afraid. You feel for the hostages. That's what you feel for, and you feel for them because you think about yourself and then you start thinking about the guys around you. When we heard about the hostages being shot, all of a sudden we were really down. It was really sad because you really think about it and you start thinking it could have happened here. The terrorists could have gone to the wrong place. Looking back on everything, I think the Games should have been cancelled.

193

The Olympics in Review

The Road to Munich

Date	Score	Opponent	High Scorer	Date	Score	Opponent	High Scorer
July 21	80-46	Hawaii All Stars	Dwight Jones 16	Aug. 16	76-65	Pro All Stars (Buffalo)	D. Jones 21
July 26	79-41	Hawaii All Stars	Tom Henderson 14 Jim Brewer 14	Aug.27 Aug. 28	66-35 81-55	Czechoslovakia Australia	Henderson 16 Ratleff 18
July 29	95-42	Kaneohe MAS	Henderson 16	Aug. 29	67-48	Cuba	D. Jones 18
Aug. 2	89-57	Kaneohe MAS	Mike Bantom 17	Aug. 30	61-54	Brazil	Henderson 12
Aug. 10	65-52	Ex-Olympians (Dayton)	D. Jones 18	Sept. 1	96-31	Egypt	Bantom 17
Aug. 11	84-71	Pro-All Stars (Louisville)	Ed Ratleff 15	Sept. 2 Sept. 3	72-56 99-33	Spain Japan	Bantom 11 Bantom 18
Aug. 13	65-63	Pro All Stars (Los Angeles)	Henderson 17	Sept. 7	68-38	Italy	Jim Forbes 14
Aug. 15	82-76	ABA All Stars (Greensboro)	Doug Collins 32	Sept. 9	50-51†	U.S.S.R.	Brewer-Henderson 9
				†Under I.O.C. Review as Protest			

1972 Olympic Basketball Team

No.	Player	Position	Age	Hgt.	Wt.	Home	School (Graduation)
4	Kenny Davis	G	23	6'1	179	Georgetown, KY	Marathon Oil (Georgetown 1971)
5	Doug Collins	G	20	6'6	170	Benton, IL	Illinois State 1973
6	Tom Henderson	G	20	6'3	190	Bronx, NY	San Jacinto J.C. 1972 (Hawaii 1974)
7	Mike Bantom	F	20	6'8	205	Philadelphia , PA	St. Josephs 1973
8	Bob Jones	F	20	6'9	210	Charlotte, NC	North Carolina 1974
9	Dwight Jones	C	20	6'9	210	Houston, TX	Houston 1974
10*	John Brown	F	20	6'8	220	Dixon, MO	Missouri 1974
11	Jim Brewer	C-F	20	6'7	215	Maywood, IL	Minnesota 1973
12	Tom Burleson	C	20	7'4	230	Newland, NC	North Carolina State 1974
13	Tom McMillen	C-F	20	6'11	210	Mansfield, PA	Maryland 1974
14	Kevin Joyce	G	21	6'2	190	Merrick, L.I., NY	South Carolina 1973
15	Ed Ratleff	G-F	22	6'6	195	Columbus, OH	Long Beach State 1973

* Due to a broken foot, Brown was replaced by Jim Forbes, 6'7; from Univ. of Texas (El Paso)

COACH: Henry P. Iba, Oklahoma State U.

Assistant Coach: Don Haskins, U. of Texas-El Paso

Assistant Coach: John Bach, Penn State U.

Manager: M.K. "Bill" Summers, Brownstown, IN   Chairman, 1972 US Olympic Basketball Committee

Assistant Manager: Herbert J. Mols, Park Schoool, Amherst, NY

Trainer: Albert C. "Whitey" Gwynne, West Virginia U.

Game Officials: Naz Servido, Erie, PA; Jim Bain, Decatur, IL; Selected to work Olympic Games in Munich.

Olympic Results

GROUP A

66	USA	Czechoslovakia 35
105	Cuba	Egypt 64
110	Brazil	Japan 55
79	Spain	Australia 74
81	USA	Australia 55
110	Brazil	Egypt 84
74	Cuba	Spain 53
74	Czechoslovakia	Japan 61
67	USA	Cuba 48
72	Brazil	Spain 69
78	Japan	Egypt 73
69	Czechoslovakia	Australia 68
61	USA	Brazil 54
72	Spain	Egypt 58
92	Australia	Japan 76
77	Cuba	Czechoslovakia 65
96	USA	Egypt 31
84	Cuba	Australia 70
87	Spain	Japan 76
83	Brazil	Czechoslovakia 82
72	USA	Spain 56
94	Czechoslovakia	Egypt 64
75	Australia	Brazil 69
108	Cuba	Japan 63
99	USA	Japan 33
74	Czechoslovakia	Spain 70
89	Australia	Egypt 66
64	Cuba	Brazil 63

GROUP B

94	Russia	Senegal 52
85	Yugoslavia	Italy 78
81	Puerto Rico	West Germany 74
90	Poland	Phillipines 75
87	Russia	West Germany 63
92	Puerto Rico	Phillipines 72
85	Yugoslavia	Poland 64
92	Italy	Senegal 56
95	Poland	Senegal 59
79	Russia	Italy 66
79	Puerto Rico	Yugoslavia 74
93	West Germany	Phillipines 74
94	Russia	Poland 64
68	Italy	West Germany 57
117	Yugoslavia	Phillipines 76
92	Puerto Rico	Senegal 57
81	Yugoslavia	West Germany 56
68	Phillipines	Senegal 62
71	Italy	Poland 59
100	Russia	Puerto Rico 87
73	Yugoslavia	Senegal 57
67	West Germany	Poland 65
111	Russia	Phillipines 80
71	Italy	Puerto Rico 54
85	Puerto Rico	Poland 83
74	Russia	Yugoslavia 67
101	Italy	Phillipines 81
72	West Germany	Senegal 62

SEMI-FINALS

68	USA	Italy 38
67	Russia	Cuba 61
66	Yugoslavia	Czechoslovakia 63
87	Puerto Rico	Brazil 88

GROUP STANDINGS
GROUP A

	W	L
United States	7	0
Cuba	6	1
Brazil	4	3
Czechoslovakia	4	3
Australia	3	4
Spain	3	4
Japan	1	6
Egypt	0	7

GROUP B

	W	L
Russia	7	0
Italy	5	2
Yugoslavia	5	2
Puerto Rico	5	2
West Germany	3	4
Poland	2	5
Phillipines	1	6
Senegal	0	7

USA SCORING–ALL GAMES

	G	FG	F	Pts.
Dwight Jones	9	34	18	86
Mike Banton	9	31	13	75
Tom Henderson	9	35	3	73
Doug Collins	9	24	17	65
Tom McMillen	9	25	10	60
Jim Brewer	9	21	18	60
Ed Ratleff	9	27	5	59
Jim Forbes	9	29	0	58
Bob Jones	8	15	11	41
Kevin Joyce	9	17	6	40
Tom Burleson	8	10	10	30
Ken Davis	7	5	4	14
	—	—	—	—
USA Total	9	278	115	661
Opponents Total	9	161	92	414

FINAL STANDINGS

(15)	2	Senegal	Egypt 0
(13)	82	Phillipines	Japan 73
(11)	84	Spain	West Germany 83
(9)	91	Australia	Poland 83
(7)	87	Brazil	Czechoslovakia 69
(5)	86	Yugoslavia	Puerto Rico 70
(3)	66	Cuba	Italy 65
(1)	51	Russia	USA 50

CHAMPIONSHIP GAME

Russia (51)	G	FT	Pts.		United States (50)	G	FT	Pts.
Polivoda	0	0-0	0		Davis	0	0-0	0
Paulauskas	0	3-4	3		Collins	1	6-6	8
Skakandidz	2	4-8	8		Henderson	4	1-2	9
Sharm'edov	1	2-4	4		Bantom	1	0-2	2
Boloshev	2	0-0	4		R. Jones	0	0-0	0
Edeshko	0	0-0	0		D. Jones	2	2-4	6
S. Belov	8	4-6	20		Forbes	1	0-0	2
Korkia	1	2-2	4		Brewer	3	3-4	9
Dvorni	0	0-0	0		Burleson	0	0-0	0
Volnov	0	0-0	0		McMillen	1	0-0	2
A. Belov	3	2-4	8		Joyce	3	0-0	6
Kovalenko	0	0-0	0		Ratleff	3	0-0	6
Total	17	17-28	51		Total	19	12-18	50

Russia .. 26 25 —51
USA.... 21 29 —50

Total fouls—Russia 25, USA 26   Attendance —6500

About the Authors

Mike Brewster, a graduate of the Columbia University School of Journalism, has worked as a sportswriter, business writer, and corporate marketing professional. He is the author of the books *Driving Change: The UPS Approach to Business, Unaccountable,* and *King of Capital: Sandy Weill and the Making of Citigroup.* He lives in New York City and plays basketball in Riverside Park.

Taps Gallagher, a native New Yorker, received his M.A. from St. John's University in New York and his J.D. degree from Loyola University of Chicago. He has been involved with basketball his entire life as a player, coach, referee and historian. *Stolen Glory* is his first published work. He now resides in Clarendon Hills, Illinois and is still a New York Knicks fan.